innovative
FABRIC
imagery for
QUILTS

Must-Have Guide to Transforming & Printing Your Favorite Images on Fabric

Cyndy Lyle Rymer with
Lynn Koolish

C&T PUBLISHING

Text and Artwork copyright © 2007
by Cyndy Lyle Rymer

Artwork copyright © 2007 by C&T Publishing, Inc.

Publisher: Amy Marson

Editorial Director: Gailen Runge

Acquisitions Editor: Jan Grigsby

Editor: Lynn Koolish

Technical Editors: Rene J. Steinpress and Helen Frost

Copyeditor/Proofreader: Wordfirm Inc.

Cover Designer: Kristy Zacharias

Design Director/Book Designer: Rose Sheifer-Wright

Illustrator: Joshua Mulks

Production Coordinators: Kerry Graham and
Joshua Mulks

Photography by C&T Publishing, Inc., except as noted

Published by C&T Publishing, Inc., P.O. Box 1456,
Lafayette, CA 94549

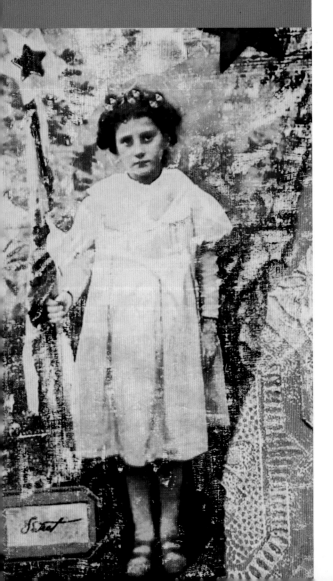

Library of Congress Cataloging-in-Publication Data
Rymer, Cyndy Lyle
    Innovative fabric imagery for quilts : must-have guide to transforming & printing your favorite images on fabric / Cyndy Lyle Rymer with Lynn Koolish.
        p. cm.
    Includes bibliographical references and index.
    ISBN-13: 978-1-57120-438-7 (paper trade : alk. paper)
    ISBN-10: 1-57120-438-5 (paper trade : alk. paper)
    1. Quilting. 2. Photographs on cloth. 3. Computer art. 4. Textile printing. I. Koolish, Lynn. II. Title.

TT835.R945 2007
746.46--dc22

                                                2007006770

Printed in China
10 9 8 7 6 5 4 3 2 1

Contents

Preface

A decade after the first inexpensive digital cameras appeared, and 8 years after C&T Publishing brought out its first book on using computers and printers to put images on fabric, what are quilt artists creating today with digital technology? That was the question on our minds when we put out a call for entries for a new book and a special exhibit on Innovative Fabric Imagery, to be presented by C&T Publishing at the Fall 2007 International Quilt Market and Festival in Houston. As digital quilt artists ourselves, we expected to be surprised. But we still weren't prepared for the breadth and quality of the entries we received.

Quilts that express a highly personal creative vision. Quilts that make a political statement. Quilts that will amuse, inspire, even astonish you—you'll find all those and more in this collection. While the works of art shown in this book cover an immense variety of styles and subjects, they all share one common element: digital technology played a vital part in their creation.

We'd like to thank all the quilt artists who submitted their work, especially those who created projects for this book. We invite you to enjoy their fabulous work and to try out some of the techniques for yourself. If you're new to printing on fabric, we've included projects with step-by-step instructions, as well as tips and techniques you can use to create similar projects or to learn a specific technique. You may want to refer to our previous books, *Photo Fun* and *More Photo Fun*, for more techniques and projects.

Most of all, we encourage you to let your creativity loose and have fun.

Lynn Koolish

C&T Publishing

Introduction

To sew or play with images in Photoshop? That is the tough question I puzzle over whenever I have some spare time. If you are just getting into printing photos and other images on fabric, beware: It's addictive. There are nights when I have trouble getting to sleep because I am thinking about what I want to work on the next morning. I'll finally start drifting off, not at all sure how I want to arrange images in a wallhanging or quilt. But miracle of miracles, the next morning I wake up with a great design idea and rush into my studio to get to work (okay, I make a cup of tea first). I'll be honest— sometimes those great ideas don't work out exactly as planned, and I get frustrated because I have "wasted" a precious sheet or two of pretreated fabric. It's all part of the learning curve, however, and any time or materials spent making art are always a good investment.

I am a true Photoshop Elements junkie and can spend hours playing on my computer with the color, size, and shape of a photo. Filters are so much fun to experiment with—in just seconds, your photo can be transformed into a still-life painting.

Why settle for sunglasses when flowers are so much more expressive?

A bowl of limes and a vase of simple white daisies is transformed with Photoshop Elements' *Artistic/Palette Knife* filter.

You can then venture into the realm of layers and stack multiple images to make collages.

Don't let the technology scare you off. It's impossible to break anything, so feel free to experiment. Take some classes through your local adult education center. Go online to see what's available. Photoshop Elements users can check out www.photoshopelementsuser.com. Sign up for online classes or for the newsletter, which offers great instructional articles.

In *More Photo Fun,* we introduced a variety of photo-editing software packages. One of our favorites, Kaleidoscope Kreator, has been updated. What you can do with this software is nothing short of magic. The creator of the software, Jeanie Sumrall-Ajero, made *Gramsie* (page 48), the wonderful quilt that celebrates her grandmother.

Take a few moments to look through the galleries in this book (pages 57–91), and you will see that soft tech and high tech get along famously. The quilt artists featured use a variety of cameras, software programs, printers, and printing services.

There are many ways to get your photos or other images onto fabric. Although this book focuses on using an all-in-one (inkjet printer/copier/scanner), there are other methods if you don't own or plan to purchase an all-in-one. *Quilted Memories* (see Resources, page 94), by Lesley Riley, inspired me to try my hand at acrylic medium transfers—transferring photos onto fabric using Golden matte medium and photo paper or inkjet transparencies. This hands-on process yields a different texture and feel and a romantic, almost mysterious, appearance. It's great to have options when creativity strikes!

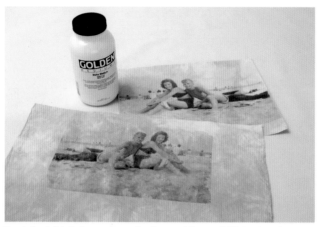

Hand-dyed fabric is used as a background for an inkjet-printed photo (top) and a acrylic-transferred photo.

If you own an all-in-one, a computer, a digital camera, basic photo-editing software, and a sewing machine, you will find that there is never enough time to experiment with all that is possible. Try working small, as

Detail of *Chic Music* (page 72)

in the *Chic Music* series which explores lyrics by female musicians. (pages 55–56 and 72–73). Pick a theme and explore a variety of techniques. Think about doing a series based on your favorite books, childhood memories (yours or your children's), favorite places, the homes you've lived in . . .

If you do own an all-in-one, but the idea of using a computer and photo-editing software gives you sweaty palms, keep in mind that you don't have to connect your all-in-one to a computer to get great images. You can use the machine's copy function to create wonderful images. You can convert a color photo to black and white simply by pushing the Black Copy button instead of the Color button. You can create an entire collage of images, text, and three-dimensional objects on the scanner bed. (On most all-in-ones, the cover can be lifted completely off, allowing you to place just about anything on the scanner bed.)

One word of advice: Carry a camera with you everywhere. I often forget, and of course that's when I see the most amazing things. One day, I saw a woman pushing a pram full of elderly Yorkshire terriers, with two more walking alongside her. The same day, I saw an older couple pushing a home-made "stroller" for their parrot. And I didn't have my camera. Aargh! Make sure you recharge your battery often, and get out there and have fun!

Cyndy Lyle Rymer

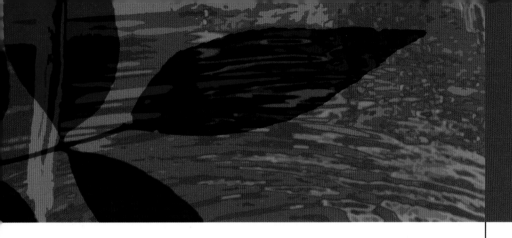

Basics

When printing images on fabric, there are many tools and supplies you *can* use, but you *really* only need a few supplies to get started: an inkjet printer, pretreated fabric, and your images. If you own or have access to an all-in-one—a machine that scans, copies, and prints—you don't even *need* a computer. Just place an image or a three-dimensional object onto the scanner bed and copy/print it directly onto your fabric.

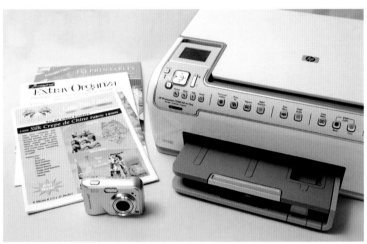

Basic supplies

Digital Camera

You don't have to use a digital camera, but the cost of the simpler digital cameras is no longer prohibitive. Owning one will expand your creative horizons. Most digital cameras come with some form of photo-editing software, so you can fix many problems, such as red eye, while you have fun playing with your photos. Look for a camera that includes the following:

- A minimum of 3- to 5-megapixel images—more is better
- Memory cards that have a storage capacity of at least 128 megabytes—the more storage capacity, the more photos you can take
- The same type of connection port as your computer—serial, USB, or IR
- An AC adapter for transferring images to your computer without using the camera's battery power
- A macro or zoom feature that allows you to zoom in close to a subject, such as a flower

If you don't want to purchase a digital camera but you *do* want to play with your images on your computer, ask for a CD of your photos in addition to the prints when you have your film processed.

Copyright Alert: Naturally, your own photos are the best source of images to print on fabric. The second-best source is the Internet, where there are many copyright-free images just waiting to be discovered. Make sure any image you use from a Web site indicates that it is copyright free. You can also pay a small fee to use photos from stock photography sites, such as PhotoSpin.com or iStockphoto.com. You will be amazed at what you can find on these sites. See page 31 for more sources of free photos.

Fabrics for Printing

You can prepare your own fabric sheets for printing, or you can purchase pretreated fabric sheets. The easiest choice is to buy the pretreated, ready-to-use sheets. The least-expensive choice is to prepare your own fabric sheets. Pretreated fabric sheets come in a variety of fabrics. They also come with a plain paper backing, a fusible backing that is ready to fuse to fabric or paper, or a sticky back that you simply press to fabric or paper (see Resources, page 94). Be sure to read the manufacturer's instructions for using and caring for printed images.

Bubble Jet Set 2000, manufactured by the C. Jenkins Necktie & Chemical Company, enables you to treat your own fabric so you can use just about any natural fiber, including hand-dyes (cotton, silk, rayon, and so on). One 32-ounce bottle will treat about 50 sheets of fabric. Follow the manufacturer's instructions for preparing your own sheets and for rinsing after printing. (The company also makes a special rinse formula.)

If you want to make your own fabric sheets, you'll need to back them so they feed through the printer. Suggested backing materials include freezer paper, full-size adhesive label sheets, or contact paper. After printing, just peel off the backing. You can use the backing sheets several times before they lose their stickiness. If you plan to fuse the printed fabric, iron paper-backed fusible web to the fabric before printing. This often provides enough stability and saves you a step.

Hand-dyed fabrics make interesting backgrounds.

If you want to prepare your own sheets of lightweight fabric, such as silk or organza, quilt artist Carol Clasper suggests spraying a sheet of acetate with temporary adhesive. Then cut your fabric about $1/4''$ larger all around and finger-press onto the acetate. Trim to size and print. The best part is that the acetate is reusable.

Avoiding Printer Jams

If you are having trouble with your fabric sheets, especially ones you prepare yourself, try stitching about $1/8''$ away from the leading edge of your paper-backed fabric. You can also diagonally clip the leading corners just a bit to help the sheets feed into the printer and to avoid jams.

Preserving Images

To improve the colorfastness of printed images, Lori Dvir-Djerassi, owner of ColorTextiles, suggests spraying your printed images with a fabric protector, such as Scotchgard, before using them in a quilt. Spray *lightly*—first horizontally, then vertically. The fabric will be a bit stiffer, but your images will be better protected.

Artist Charlotte Ziebarth (see page 85) sprays her images with a Krylon acrylic spray, available at art-supply stores.

Gloria Hansen (pages 29 and 59) mixes three parts water to one part white glue to make a protective coating for photos on fabric. You can soak the image in a flat tray filled with the mixture, brush it on, or use a spray bottle to spray it on. All you need is a thin coating.

All About All-in-Ones

All-in-ones are handy machines to have, and they aren't terribly expensive. You can print from your computer to an all-in-one just like you would print to any other printer. You can also use it as a scanner to scan images to your computer. With most all-in-ones, you can also print directly from many types of camera memory cards.

The true value of an all-in-one, though, is that you can copy images onto fabric without using a computer at all. Here's how:

1. Place the photo face down on the scanner bed.
2. Make a test copy on paper.
3. Feed one pretreated fabric sheet into the machine, just as you would a sheet of paper.
4. Press the *Copy* button and scroll through the print options to reduce or enlarge your image, make it lighter or darker, increase the color intensity, and so on.
5. Press the *Black* or *Color* Start button.

You can also take the cover off most machines and place just about anything that isn't liquid on the scanner bed. Cover the items with fabric or paper to provide a background, and scan/print directly onto fabric. When using items that are messy or that could scratch the all-in-one's glass, place an acetate or transparency sheet (you can find both at office-supply stores) on the glass before arranging your items. Make test copies on plain paper first to make sure you like the arrangement.

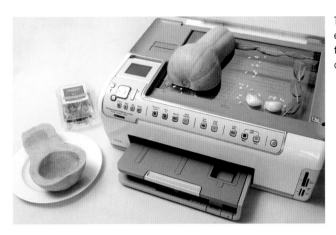

Take off the top and experiment with three-dimensional objects.

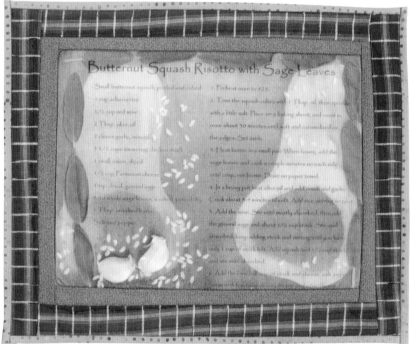

Create a kitchen quilt by stacking a recipe printed on a transparency, a layer of organza, vegetables, and a backing.

Reducing and Enlarging

Every printer is different, but one of the buttons you will likely love the most will be called something like *Reduce/Enlarge*. You can use this to print your photos in standard photo sizes, such as 4″ × 6″ or 5″ × 7″, or to reduce or enlarge to other sizes.

Poster Printing

Some all-in-ones offer *Poster* printing under the *Reduce/Enlarge* option. This allows you to create a larger image that is printed on several sheets of fabric—up to 25 sheets. When you print directly from a photo placed on the scanner bed of your all-in-one, the sheets are printed with a ⅛″ allowance on all sides. For a slightly wider seam allowance, place the photo about ½″ away from the appropriate corner of the machine.

To join the sections of your printed photo, pin and then carefully sew the sheets together. Another option for joining the sections is to iron fusible web to the back of each sheet with seam allowances intact. Trim the seam allowances, position each sheet with the edges butted together onto a base fabric, and fuse onto the base. See *Clover Lake* (page 43) and *Falling Leaves* (page 46) for ideas on using poster printing.

Butt the edges of the photo together, then fuse to a base fabric.

Note: Some printers have a poster function built into the Print Properties (see Larger Images on pages 18–19), or if you have photo-editing software, you can split up your photo in the software and enlarge each section (see page 30 for detailed instructions).

If you prefer, you can manually cut a printed photo into sections, then print the sections one at a time on separate pretreated fabric sheets using the *Enlarge>Fill Page* option on your all-in-one.

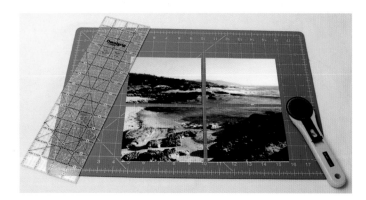

Test Prints Save Ink and Fabric Sheets

When printing on fabric, always make test prints on paper so you don't waste ink or fabric sheets. From *Copy Quality,* choose the *Fast* or *Draft* option. Copy in black and white to determine whether you need to reduce or enlarge a photo and whether the placement and arrangement are what you want. Once everything is set, try a color print on paper. Although the color will be deeper and truer when you print using *Normal* or *Best,* the *Fast* or *Draft* print will give you a good idea of what the color will look like. Save the test prints for laying out potential designs.

Scanning

A scanner takes a picture of whatever is on the scanner bed and sends the image to your computer. You can then use software to manipulate the images. An all-in-one usually includes scanning capabilities, or you can use a stand-alone flatbed scanner.

Scanners, whether stand-alone or part of an all-in-one, often come with software that offers a number of ways for you to manipulate an image before you make the final scan.

- Rotate the image.
- Crop or resize the image.
- Lighten or darken the image.
- Sharpen the image (but know that you will never be able to work miracles on a photo that is totally out of focus).
- Adjust the color.
- Change the resolution. Use a resolution of at least 150 dots per inch (dpi) or higher for printing on fabric.
- Invert the colors: light to dark, dark to light.
- Mirror the image.

When you want to scan several photos on the scanner bed at the same time, group them according to size. Scan all close-ups together, and group longer-distance shots. If you have several images you want to reduce or enlarge, group them and use the *Resize* option.

How to Scan Using a Scanner or All-in-One

There are a number of ways to use a scanner, including pressing the Scan button on the scanner or all-in-one, using the scanning software that came with the machine, or starting from your photo-editing software, as described below.

1. Position the photo(s) or other artwork face down on the scanner glass. If you are scanning anything that might scratch or otherwise harm the scanner bed (such as shells), place a piece of acetate on the scanner bed to protect it. Covering the scanner bed with plastic wrap adds an interesting effect, but it may not create the image you had in mind.

2. Open the program you use to scan. (In Photoshop Elements, go to *File>Import*.) Scroll through the pop-up list and choose your scanner or all-in-one.

3. Choose a resolution of at least 150 dpi for printing on fabric. If you plan to print a larger image, increase the number to 300–600 so the quality isn't adversely affected.

4. Select *Scan* or *Acquire* from the *File* menu, or push the Scan button on the machine itself.

5. Save the image to your computer as a jpeg or tiff file.

A Note on File Formats

Most digital images are stored either as a jpeg (.jpg) or as a tiff (.tif). Many digital cameras store images as jpegs. You can use either file format. Tiff files store more details and are larger, taking more disk space on your computer. Jpeg files are smaller, but store less detail. Experiment with both formats and see which works best for you.

Storing Your Photos

It's easy to store your photos on your computer's hard drive, but this uses a lot of space. To avoid overloading your computer and potential loss, burn your images onto CDs or DVDs, or use an online storage company, such as pictures.aol.com, smugmug.com, or pixagogo.com.

Photo-Editing Software

Basic photo-editing software is often included with the purchase of a digital camera or an all-in-one inkjet printer.

Adobe Photoshop Elements (available for PCs and Macs) and Corel Paint Shop Pro Photo (only available for PCs) are reasonably priced photo-editing programs designed for casual users. Many other programs are available, but these two are the ones used most often by the artists in this book.

Try It for Free

A free 30-day trial version of Adobe Photoshop Elements is available for download at www.ctpub.com. Look for the Adobe icon.

For a basic but free and very user-friendly photo-editing program, go to www.picasa.com. You can crop, adjust highlights or contrast, and convert your photos to sepia or soft focus. It's also great for e-mailing photos and sharing photo albums online.

Once you have installed photo-editing software, spend some time playing with it and checking out the tutorials or the *Hints* or *Recipe* files. You can also access the online *Help* file. For Photoshop Elements users, www.photoshopelementsuser.com offers online tutorials, as well as a newsletter with articles that delve into all the fabulous things you can do with Photoshop Elements. It's worth the subscription price!

Specialty Software

Many specialty photo-editing software programs are available, often at a very reasonable cost. Some of the software programs that we've used and liked are:

- Kaleidoscope Kreator (see page 49) to turn images into kaleidoscopes
- PhotoMontage to create an image made of many small images
- Print Shop to print long banners
- Panorama Maker to stitch a series of photos into one single image

We've listed these in Resources (page 94), but shop around as well, and you'll find many intriguing programs.

Photoshop Elements

Note: All projects included in this book give instructions for using Photoshop Elements. New versions of photo-editing software are released by the manufacturers on a regular basis. Functionality is generally consistent, although there may be some variations between the different versions and computers. When we began writing this book, we were using Photoshop Elements Version 4.0 for the PC. As we were working on the book, Adobe released Version 5.0 for the PC, while the Macs continued to use Version 4. If you are using another photo-editing program, consult the manual or *Help* file to find similar functionality.

Photoshop Elements includes basic tools that make photo editing fun and easy. It takes a little time to learn to use the tools, but there's a tremendous amount you can do with just a little bit of knowledge. The following is a taste to get you started.

Photoshop has two parts. The *Organizer* is a catalog of photos on your computer. The *Editor* is where the action is. There are several ways to access the *Editor,* depending on how you start the program. Regardless of how you start, select *Edit>Go to Standard Edit* or *Edit and Enhance Photos.*

Getting Around in Photoshop Elements

Most of the tools in the *Editor* are straightforward and perform one function when you click on them. However, some of the tools have a submenu that appears when you click on them. If you aren't sure what a tool icon means, simply place your cursor on the icon, and a text box will appear with the name of the tool. Most of the tools also have options that are available in the *Options* bar.

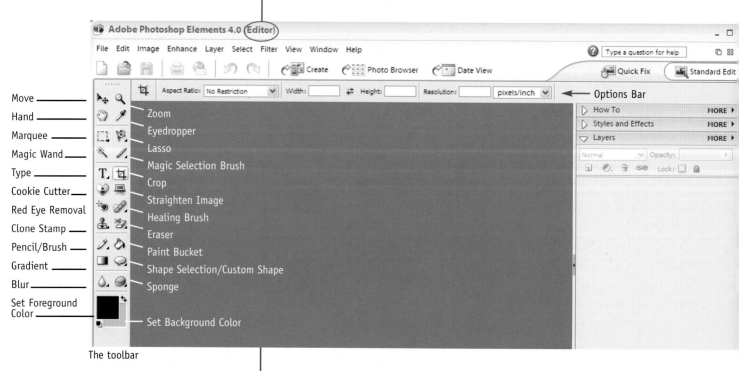

The toolbar

If you're just getting started with Photoshop Elements, try using the following few tools first. When you're ready for more, check out the Appendix (pages 92–93) for more on using the toolbar.

Move tool Use it to move images from place to place or from one image frame to another image frame. (For example, see page 16 for combining images.)

Zoom tool Click on a section of an image to enlarge it so you can see the details better.

Hand tool A little hand cursor appears, allowing you to move an image within the frame. This is helpful when the image is larger than the frame, and you can't see the whole thing at once.

Marquee tool A very useful tool for selecting (or deselecting) parts of an image (see page 14). The choices are *Rectangular* or *Elliptical*. Use this tool in combination with the *Crop tool* (page 14) or when copying and pasting (page 16).

Use the *Elliptical Marquee* tool to make a circular selection.

Crop tool Use this tool to trim or select portions of your image. In the menu bar, you can change the *Aspect Ratio* to set the height and width of the crop (especially useful if you want to crop a number of images to the same size), or you can simply drag your mouse to define the outline of the crop.

Crop to the good part
(no kittens were harmed).

The Most Important Tip for Using Photoshop

When you don't like something you have done, don't panic. Go up to *Edit,* and at the top menu bar you'll see *Undo* or *Revert.* Click on *Undo* to go back to the image you just altered. Click on *Revert* if you want to go back to the way the file was the last time you saved it.

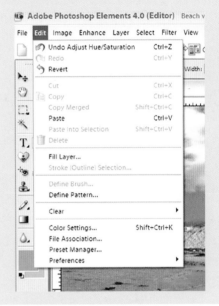

Enlarging, Cropping, and Combining Images

When you start working with Photoshop Elements, you'll most likely want to change the size of your images and combine different images into one file.

Many thanks to Gloria Hansen for the following tips about sizing, cropping, and combining images in one file to save space when printing. The following specifics are for Photoshop Elements, but other photo-editing software will have similar functionality.

Enlarging an Image Without Quality Loss

1. Open the image you want to enlarge and save it with a new file name.
2. Go to *Image>Resize>Image Size*. Under *Image Size,* insert either the width or the height that you want for your final image. Keep the *Scale Styles*, *Constrain Proportions*, and *Resample Image* boxes checked.
3. Here's the trick: From the drop-down menu, select *Bicubic Sharper,* which will help retain the image quality.

Cropping Your Image to an Exact Size

Say you have an image that is 9″ × 12″, but you want to print it onto fabric at 8″ × 10″ or 4″ × 6″. Here's an easy way to crop exactly to the size you want.

1. Open the image you want to crop and save it with a new file name.
2. Select the *Crop tool*.
3. In the *Options* bar under the main menu, enter the desired width and height, or select an option in the *Aspect Ratio* box. Enter "300" and select "pixels/inch" from the drop-down menu as the resolution.
4. Use your mouse to select a portion of your image. When you let go of the mouse button, you'll see a marquee or a dashed outline (sometimes called "marching ants"). Use your mouse to move the outline to any location on the image or to make the crop larger or smaller.
5. When you press *Enter*, the image will crop to your exact specifications. No matter how small or large an area you've selected, the resulting crop will always be the size you indicated.

The *Crop tool* will remain set to the same options until you clear them by setting the *Aspect Ratio* to *No Restriction*.

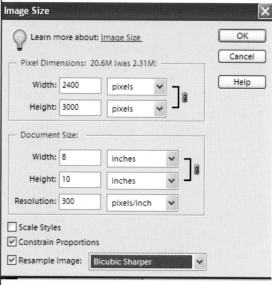

Resizing options

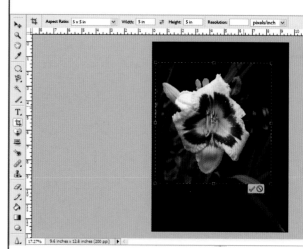

Crop tool and cropping options

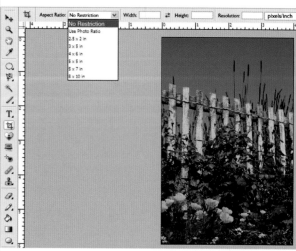

Clearing cropping options

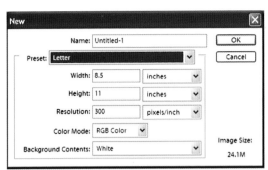
Create a new, blank file.

Creating New Blank Files

When you want to combine images onto one page, you need a new, blank file. Choose *File>New>Blank File*. From there, you can either select a preset size or enter your own custom size.

Tip

Three buttons or tools that appear at the extreme top right above your working screen are particularly helpful when working with multiple images. *Cascade Windows* lets you see multiple images on your working screen. *Automatically Tile Windows* makes images on your screen more orderly—all the photos are there if you want them, but in an abbreviated fashion. *Maximize Mode* enlarges just the chosen image.

Cascade Windows
Automatically Tile Windows
Maximize Windows

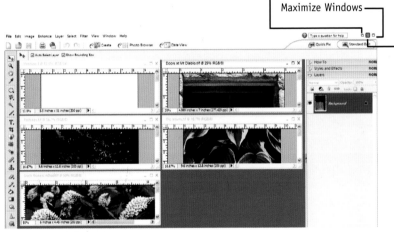
Automatically Tile Windows

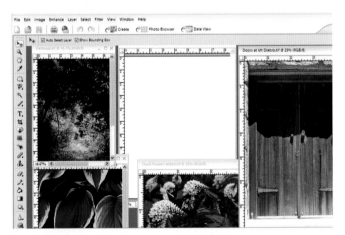
Cascade Windows

Megapixels, Resolution, and DPI

A pixel is essentially a dot of color stored either in your camera or on the computer. A megapixel is one million pixels. The more pixels in an image, the clearer (or bigger) the image is when you look at it on your computer (that's why you want to buy a camera with the largest megapixel images that makes sense for your budget).

Resolution determines the quality of your printed image and is measured in dpi (dots per inch). The higher the resolution, the better your printed image will look. The more megapixels an image has when you shoot it, the higher the dpi can be when you print the image, resulting in a clearer, sharper, and larger picture.

Photo printed at 72 dpi.

Photo printed at 300 dpi.

Combining More Than One Image on a Page

No one likes to waste fabric, and there's no reason to print one small photo at a time on your fabric when you can arrange your photos to fit your fabric sheet. Gloria Hansen uses a method that gives you control over exactly what images you want to print.

1. Open a new 8½″ x 11″ file (or whatever size you want to print to). We'll call this New File. *Note:* When planning to combine images, be sure to first note the dpi of each of the images you want to combine in one document. Then, when creating the new file, set the resolution so it matches the resolution of your images.

2. Open your first image. We'll call this first one Image 1. Select the *Move tool*, hold the mouse down, and drag Image 1 into New File. When you let go of the mouse button, Image 1 will be placed in New File.
   If Image 1 opened to the full size of your monitor, covering New File, resize it to make it smaller. On a PC, do this by grabbing any edge of the window and dragging inward. On a Mac, grab the bottom right corner and drag in.

3. Continue in this manner, opening the next image, resizing it so you can see New File, and dragging the next image onto New File. *Note:* You can easily resize any image placed into the 8½″ × 11″ document by holding down the Shift key (to constrain the proportions) and dragging inward. This works best when making the image smaller.

Drag images with the *Move tool*.

An alternative is to copy and paste Image 1 in place. While in Image 1, go to *Select>All*. You'll see a dashed outline around the entire image. Next, choose *Edit>Copy*. Then go to New File and choose *Edit>Paste*. Image 1 is now placed in New File.

4. Repeat with each image. Open the image and either drag it or copy/paste it into New File.

5. To arrange the images in New File, click on each image and place it where you want it.

Tip

When arranging images on a page, you may need to resize or rotate some to get them to fit better. Here's an easy way to do both.

1. After you have placed your images in New File, click on the image you want to change.

2. Place your mouse on a corner and drag to make the image larger or smaller. (Note: Hold down the Shift key while dragging to constrain the proportions of the image so you don't inadvertently pull it out of shape.)

3. To rotate an image, move your cursor to a corner handle, going a bit diagonally past the handle. You'll see a curved line with an arrow on both ends. Once you see that icon, drag your mouse to rotate the image, then press Enter. You can also rotate by going to *Image>Rotate* and selecting one of the options.

Color, Contrast, and Saturation

There are endless ways to manipulate the appearance of your photos by adjusting the color, contrast, saturation, brightness, and much, much more. Start by saving your image with a new file name. Then select *Enhance* from the menu bar and experiment. For color and saturation, choose *Adjust Color>Adjust Hue/Saturation*. For contrast, select *Adjust Lighting>Brightness/Contrast*. Remember that you can *Undo, Revert* (page 13), or just start over with a new copy of the image.

Filter Fun

Using photo-editing filters brings out the inner artist in all of us. If you use a photo-editing program for nothing else, you've gotten your money's worth. You can get to *Filter* either through a drop-down menu in the top menu bar or from *Layer*. Filters provide instant gratification—just click on one, and the image is transformed. If you like what you see, click *OK*; otherwise, click *Cancel*. There are also options within many of the filters. For example, in *Distort>Glass,* you can change the amount of distortion, smoothness, and type of glass: *Blocks, Canvas, Frosted,* or *Tiny Lens.*

The *Filter* toolbar in *Layer*

The same photo was altered using the *Distort>Glass* filter with high distortion and smoothness values and the *Frosted Glass* setting.

Using Filters

The fun really begins when you combine filters and other photo-editing functionality. In the following example, a photo of fireworks goes through a transformation into a marble.

Original fireworks photo

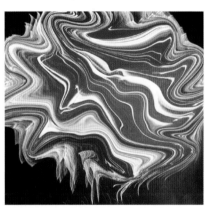

Fireworks photo modified with the *Distort>Liquify* filter

The color of the modified fireworks photo was changed using *Adjust Hue* and a circular *Cookie Cutter* (page 92) was used to crop the image into a circle.

A Little About Layers

An entire book could be written about what you can cook up once you venture into the land of layers. Layers allow you to stack images on top of one another. What makes them endlessly fascinating is that you control the opacity (transparency) of each layer.

Following is an example of how two images can be combined. You are probably starting to see how the possibilities are endless. Experiment and have fun. For more help, refer to the Photoshop Elements *User Guide* that comes with the software, subscribe to www.photoshopelementsuser.com, or buy a tutorial type of book.

The clock on the left was moved to the sunset on the right using the *Move* tool, then the opacity of the clock was decreased using *Layer*.

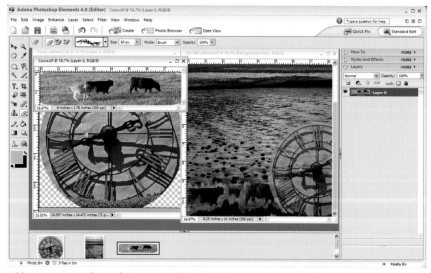

Add some cows and use the *Eraser* tool (page 93) to begin revealing the sunset layer beneath.

Print It!

The size of your image is perfect, the crop is good, the color is beautiful, you've made your test copy on paper (page 10), you have your pre-treated fabric sheets (page 8), and you are ready to print on fabric.

Set the copy quality to *Normal* or *Best* and double-check the orientation—portrait or landscape—and you're good to go. Remove any other sheets of paper from the paper feeder and print one sheet of fabric at a time.

Tip

Fabric sheets may have lint or loose threads on them. Remove any specks of lint and cut off—don't pull—any loose threads before you load the fabric sheet into the printer.

Larger Images

So what do you do if you want to print an image larger than the standard 8½″ × 11″? In addition to the poster-printing function that's built into some all-in-ones, you may also have a poster-printing option in your photo-editing software. Before sending a file to the printer, open *Print Properties*. From there, you may have to poke around a bit. In some software, the poster-printing option might be under *Finishing*; on others, it might be under *Features*. Once you find the correct option, select the number of pages. You will definitely want to do a test run on paper in *Draft* or *Fast* mode first to see how the image gets split up.

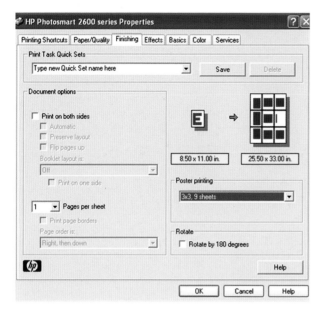

Poster printing

If you want complete control over dividing the image, see Gloria Hansen's *Ocean Sunset* (page 29) for complete instructions.

If printing directly on larger fabric sheets is your preferred style, a more expensive option is to purchase a printer that can print larger sheets. Both Hewlett-Packard and Epson offer desktop printers that can print up to 13″ × 19″ fabric sheets. Not only can you print larger images, but these larger printers also offer poster-printing options that allow you to start with a 5″ × 5″ image and print it at an amazing 85″ × 55″.

Currently, it's difficult to find *affordable* inkjet printers that offer anything larger than 13″ × 19″ prints. Epson manufactures wider-format printers that sell for $1,000 to $5,000—and the price jumps from there. The less-expensive option is to send your image to a professional printing company (see Resources, page 94). Check individual company Web sites, as most require a CD or DVD with the image saved as a tiff file at about 300 dpi.

Printer Maintenance

For the best-quality prints, you'll need to maintain your printer. To get rid of any lines that show up when you print in *Normal* or *Best,* be sure to service your printer. (To do this, you need to connect your printer to a computer.) Each printer manufacturer and print model will be slightly different. In general, select *Print* from any program that allows you to print documents or images, such as Microsoft Word or Photoshop Elements. Then select *Properties*. From there, you may have to hunt around a bit, but what you are looking for will be something like *Services* or *Toolbox*. Select *Service This Device* and/or *Clean the Print Cartridges*. You may need to go through the process more than once.

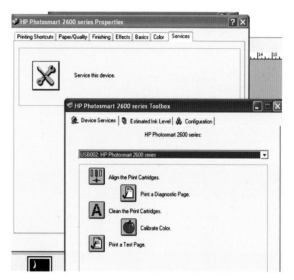

Periodically service your all-in-one by cleaning the print heads.

If you print on fabric often, it's a good idea to check your printer for loose threads or lint. Use canned air to blow out any debris that you see.

Tip

Check the status of your ink levels with *Print>Properties>Toolbox*. There is nothing more frustrating than printing on a sheet of fabric, and discovering that there isn't enough ink to get a good-quality print.

PROJECTS

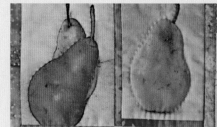

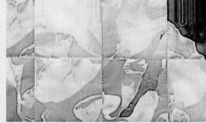

Strained But Not Drained

Jan Bode Smiley, Fort Mill, SC
Finished quilt size: 19″ × 20″

Based on the traditional Log Cabin block, this quilt makes a play on both words and images. Using photos of colanders and lots of fabrics with circles and dots, Jan worked to playfully express her frustration with the time-management-mom-business-owner-chef-CEO-chauffeur-domestic-goddess-wife-artist-all-plates-must-remain-in-the-air-at-all-times balancing conundrum that many of us juggle every day. This would be a fun idea for any collection: teapots, vases, steins, and so on.

Materials

- Photo-editing software (optional)
- 6 pretreated 8½″ × 11″ fabric sheets
- 18–20 different fabric strips with dots, a variety of widths from 1″ to 3″ × the width of the fabric
- ½ yard fabric for border and binding
- ⅔ yard fabric for backing
- 21″ × 22″ batting

Tip

For variety, vary the orientation of the shots. Jan also used subtly different fabrics as the backgrounds for the colanders, adding interest to her composition.

Photo Prep

1. Take photos of a variety of colanders or other items. (Using different styles of the same item makes this type of quilt cohesive.) Use photo-editing software to adjust the photos if needed.
2. Print images on pretreated fabric sheets.
3. Follow the manufacturer's instructions for rinsing and drying the fabric sheets.

Construction

1. Select fabric strips to add to each colander photo. Use the Log Cabin method of construction, and sew the strips to all 4 sides of each photo. Jan likes to vary her strips: straight, wedge shaped, wide, or narrow.

Tip

For additional interest, sew the strips at angles to the photograph so that the photo is no longer perfectly rectangular.

2. Arrange the blocks on your design wall.
3. Add strips, wedges, and/or slivers of some of the other dot fabrics around each of the blocks until they are all approximately the same size.
4. Continue adding wedges or strips when sewing the blocks together to make them all fit.
5. Square up the outer edges of the sewn blocks, if necessary, to make the edges straight.
6. Measure, cut, and sew border strips onto the pieced blocks.
7. Layer the quilt top, batting, and backing. Baste or pin to hold the layers together.
8. Machine quilt as desired, then trim the excess batting and backing.
9. Bind.

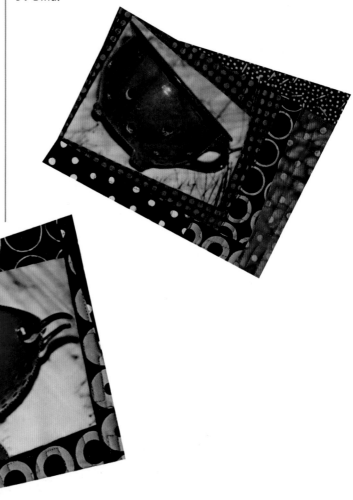

Preserving Summer

Sandra Hart, Los Gatos, CA
Finished quilt size: 20″ × 26″

An avid gardener, Sandra wanted to find a way to preserve the beauty of summer in her Santa Cruz Mountains garden. Because she is a technologically savvy quilter as well as a gardener, Sandy decided to arrange freshly picked flowers into wreaths or bouquets, photograph them, and then print the images on fabric to incorporate in wallhangings, quilts, and pillows.

Materials

- Photo-editing software (optional)
- 4 pretreated 8½" × 11" fabric sheets **OR** 1 pretreated 13" × 19" fabric sheet if you have access to a wide-format printer
- Collection of leaves, vines, and flowers fresh from the garden or flowers from a special birthday, anniversary, wedding, or birth bouquet
- ½ yard background fabric mounted on cardboard for arranging the flowers
- ¾ yard coordinating fabric for solid or pieced border and backing
- ¼ yard contrasting fabric for binding
- 22" × 28" batting

Arrange a wreath, then photograph your creation.

Photo Prep

1. Mount the background fabric on a piece of cardboard.
2. Arrange the leaves and vines to create a background for a bouquet, sheaf, or wreath.
3. Start with the larger flowers and begin adding them to the base of the wreath. Sandy used a variety of flowers from her garden. A simple wreath with just one type or color of flowers, herbs, or leaves can be beautiful. You can add ribbons, yarn, or anything else you choose to beautify your wreath.
4. Try different color combinations until you are satisfied; photograph each combination along the way and print and use your favorite or make a series of wreaths.
5. Position your creation in indirect light (avoid direct sun or dappled shade). Stand directly over the arrangement. Hold the camera level and take a number of shots, varying the settings and your distance from your floral creation.
6. Adjust the photo if needed using photo-editing software. Before you crop, make sure you leave a reasonable amount of background surrounding the arrangement. Straighten the photo and adjust the lightness, contrast, or hue.
7. Enlarge the photo. If you are using a 13" × 19" fabric sheet, resize the image to 12" × 18". If you are using 8½" × 11" fabric sheets, resize the image to approximately 8" × 10" and print on 4 fabric sheets (see pages 18–19 for options). Making the images smaller will provide generous seam allowances that make it easier to sew the fabric sheets together. If you want to make the image larger, refer to page 30 for instructions on dividing an image using Photoshop Elements.
8. Print the flower arrangement on the pretreated fabric sheets. If you are using 4 sheets of 8½" × 11" fabric, piece them carefully together.
9. Follow the manufacturer's instructions for rinsing and drying the fabric sheets.

Tip

When piecing together several fabric sheets to create one image, sew the sheets together *before* rinsing.

Construction

1. Add one or more borders around your photo. Use a coordinating stripe or border print or a pieced border. Try out different looks until you find a combination that pleases you.

Audition borders.

2. Miter the corners or add interesting piecing in the corner squares.
3. Layer the quilt top, batting, and backing. Baste or pin to hold the layers together.
4. Quilt the background in a simple grid or stipple using a neutral color of thread. Quilt the flowers and leaves with lots of beautiful threads that enhance the shapes and colors (and that hide any flaws!)
5. Bind or frame the quilted piece.

Enhance the leaves and flowers with beautiful quilting and embellishment.

Be Fruitful and Multiply

Jennifer Rounds, Walnut Creek, CA
Finished size: 16½˝ × 22˝

Jennifer positioned three fresh pears on a marble tile in a variety of poses, with white tone-on-tone fabric draped over a cookbook stand to form a background. After importing the best photos into Photoshop Elements, she bumped up the color a bit, created mirror images, resized them, and then printed them on pretreated cotton. French pear recipe names printed on organza scroll across the surface of portions of Jennifer's quilt and add interest to her composition.

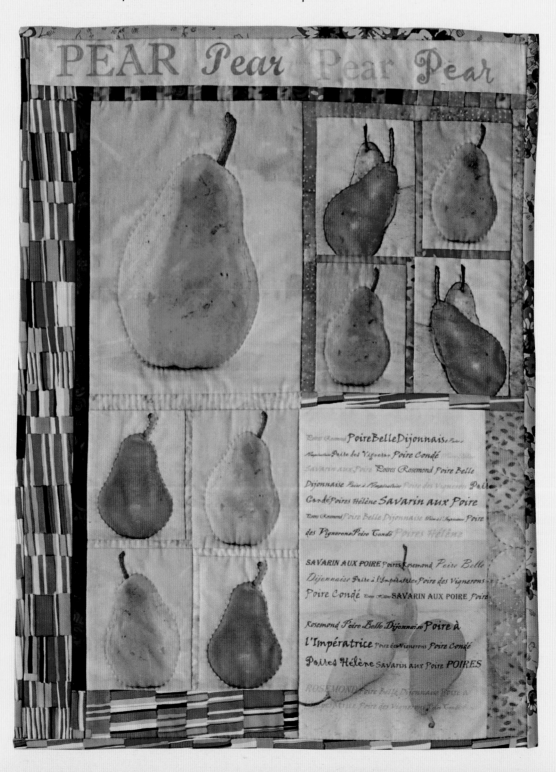

Materials

- Photo-editing software
- 4 pretreated 8½″ × 11″ fabric sheets and 2 pretreated 8½″ × 11″ sheets of Jacquard ExtravOrganza (see Resources on page 94)
- 1 yard multicolored fabric for borders, backing, and binding
- Scraps of fabric to coordinate with photos
- ⅜ yard paper-backed fusible web
- Prismacolor colored pencils
- 19″ × 24″ batting

Photo Prep

1. Open your photos with your photo-editing software.
2. Work on one photo at a time. Choose *Filter>Artistic>Poster Edges* and use the slider bars to adjust *Edge Thickness, Edge Intensity,* and/or *Posterization.* Click *OK* when you are satisfied.
3. To make the color a bit more intense and to change the color, if desired (as Jennifer did by changing the green pear in the Four-Patches to red), choose *Enhance>Adjust Color>Adjust Hue/ Saturation.* Move the slider bar to the desired intensity.
4. Choose one pear or another subject to be the main image. Resize it to 8″ × 10″.
5. To print the smaller images, open 2 new blank files (see page 15) to accommodate all the photos.
6. Use the *Move tool* (page 12–13) to drag the remaining photos onto the new files. Resize the photos as necessary by dragging the corners. Jennifer's smaller pears are approximately 4″ × 5″.
7. *Optional:* Create mirror images by choosing *Image>Rotate>Flip Horizontal.*
8. Print your images.
9. Follow the manufacturer's instructions for rinsing and drying the fabric sheets.
10. *Optional:* Use the Prismacolor pencils to further enhance the color of the images.

Original pear image

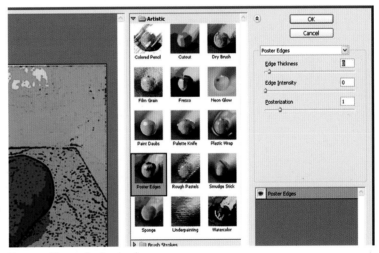

Pears with posterized edges

Construction

The quilt is a simple Four-Patch layout assembled in two columns. The left column features an 8″ × 10″ pear image and a Four-Patch of single pears (two red and two green). The right column features an 8″ x 10″ image of three pears with an ExtravOrganza overlay and a Four-Patch of single pears. Sashing strips were used liberally to compensate for the differences in image sizes in the smaller Four-Patches and to add interest to Jennifer's composition.

1. Assemble 2 Four-Patch units of smaller pear images, using sashing strips to compensate for image size differences.

2. Design and print an organza overlay for the lower-right block. Jennifer created a list of French pear recipe names in a word-processing program and used a variety of fonts and colors. She printed the text on the ExtravOrganza to create a typographic accent layer and fused it to the quilt.

3. Add sashing strips to the larger pear still life in the bottom right.

4. Lay out the overall Four-Patch, inserting accent sashing strips as needed.

5. Create a border strip for the top of the quilt. Design the strip using larger type and print on a sheet of ExtravOrganza. Fuse the overlay to the wider sashing strip and stitch it to the quilt.

6. Layer the quilt top, batting, and backing. Baste or pin to hold the layers together.

7. Machine quilt as desired, then trim the excess batting and backing.

8. Bind.

Tip

To print longer sashing strips on the ExtravOrganza, change the image orientation from *Portrait* to *Landscape* in your print dialog box before printing. Print the type on two lines.

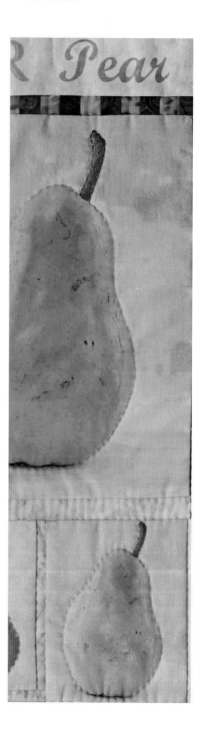

Ocean Sunset

Gloria Hansen, Hightstown, NJ
Finished size: 30″ × 24″

Ocean Sunset is fun and fast and a great project for making a memory quilt of a favorite vacation spot. This technique offers a lot of room for creative interpretations. If you don't have a favorite photo, check out sources on the Internet for beautiful, royalty-free, high-resolution images (see page 31).

Materials

- Photo-editing software
- 4 pretreated 8½″ × 11″ fabric sheets (regular or fusible)
- ⅝ yard multicolored fabric for background
- ⅓ yard each of 2 multicolored fabrics for borders
- ⅞ yard fabric for backing
- ⅓ yard fabric for binding
- 1 yard paper-backed fusible web
- 32″ × 26″ batting

Photo Prep

1. Open the photo in your photo-editing software.
2. Go to *Image>Resize*. Resize your image to 10″ × 8″ and set the resolution to 300 dpi.

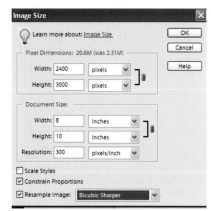

Resize image.

3. Divide the image into quarters to print on 8½″ × 11″ fabric sheets (see instructions on right).
4. Print the images on pretreated fabric sheets.
5. Follow the manufacturer's instructions for rinsing and drying the fabric sheets.

Dividing an Image to Print on 8 ½″ × 11″ Fabric Sheets

Note: Adjust your dimensions as needed for the size and orientation (*Portrait* or *Landscape*) of your original image.

1. Select *Rulers* and *Grid* from the *View* menu.
2. With the *Marquee* tool (page 13), select a quarter of the image: Start at the upper-left corner (the 0 point), and drag diagonally downward until the dashed outline indicates that you are at the 4″ mark horizontally and the 5″ mark vertically.

Use the *Marquee Tool* to make a selection.

3. Use *Edit>Copy* to copy this section of your image.
4. Open a new document by choosing *File>New>Blank File*. In the dialog box, set the image to 10″ × 8″ at 150 dpi resolution. Be sure the color is set to RGB mode.

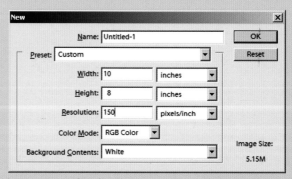

Create a new file for the top quarter of the photo.

5. Choose *Edit>Paste* to paste the quarter image into the new document.
6. Change the orientation of your document to *Landscape*. Print the image.
7. Use the *Marquee tool* to select the next quarter of your image by starting at the 4″ horizontal mark and dragging down to the 10″ mark. (If you need to deselect your marquee, go to *Select>Deselect*.) Repeat and save all four quarters of the photo in separate files.

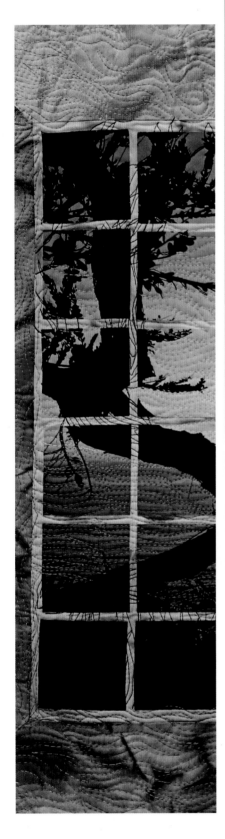

 Tip

A good way to test the color and quality of an image is to use the *Marquee tool* to select and print a small portion of the image. If you don't like what you see, you can adjust the resolution (see pages 14–15) or the color (see page 17).

Construction

1. If you aren't using fusible pretreated fabric sheets, iron paper-backed fusible web to the back of each printed fabric sheet. Remove the backing paper.
2. Cut the printed fabric sheets into equal-sized squares based on the size of your print. For example, if the print is 8″ × 10″ and you want 2″ × 2″ squares, cut 5 strips 2″ wide, then cut 4 squares from each strip. (Gloria used 2¾″ squares.)
3. Create your background, which can be a single wide piece of fabric. (Gloria used a piece of fabric she had painted.) Cut the background slightly larger than you need; you will trim it later.
4. Fuse squares into place, leaving a scant ¼″ between them.
5. If desired, add borders.
6. Layer the quilt top, batting, and backing. Baste or pin to hold the layers together.
7. Machine quilt as desired, then trim the excess batting and backing.
8. Bind.

Finding Free, Beautiful Photographs

Many Web sites offer free photographs. To find them, go to Google (www.google.com) and search on "royalty-free photographs."

One of Gloria's favorite Web sites for beautiful, free photographs is the National Oceanic and Atmospheric Administration Photo Library (www.photolib.noaa.gov). NOAA's site has more than 20,000 images, including many higher-resolution images. It includes "thousands of weather and space images, hundreds of images of our shores and coastal seas, and thousands of marine species images ranging from the great whales to the most minute plankton." Be sure to visit The Collections. If you're drawn to underwater imagery, visit The Coral Kingdom, which includes photos of coral reefs throughout the tropical ocean regions. You'll have more images than you can quilt from just this section alone!

Roses by the Square

Lynn Koolish, Berkeley, CA
Finished size: 24″ × 18³/₄″

Using the *Wave* filter in Photoshop Elements is like opening a treasure trove. You can play with different values and options until you get a look you like. There are endless possibilities. This quilt was created using the *Square* option, but try out *Sine* and *Triangle* for different effects.

Combine this filter with other filters for even more options. For example, the image for *Sun and Stars Goes Super-Nova* on (page 60) was created using the *Wave* filter after the *Twirl* filter had been applied. Of course, after you've applied the filter(s), you can adjust or enhance the color, saturation, or lighting as well.

The squares make it easy to print your image in several pieces and stitch them together if you want the image larger than your printer can print.

Materials

- Photo-editing software
- 1–4 pretreated $8\frac{1}{2}'' \times 11''$ fabric sheets
- $\frac{1}{8}$ yard pink fabric for inner border
- $\frac{1}{3}$ yard green fabric or $\frac{1}{4}$ yard each of 2 different green fabrics
  for outer border
- $\frac{3}{4}$ yard fabric for backing
- $\frac{1}{4}$ yard fabric for binding
- $26'' \times 21''$ batting

Photo Prep

1. Open the photo in your photo-editing program.

Original rose photo

2. Create the central image using *Filter>Distort>Wave*. Experiment with the settings to get a look you like. Within the *Square* option, *Wavelength* and *Amplitude* allow you to control the size of the squares and the placement of the pieces of the image within the squares.

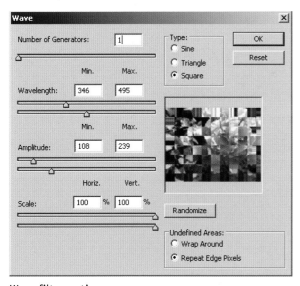

Wave filter options

Filtered rose

3. When you are finished editing, print the image on pretreated fabric sheets. If you want the image to be larger than $8\frac{1}{2}'' \times 11''$, divide the image into quarters (see page 30).

4. If you printed multiple sheets, sew them together along the lines created by the squares.

5. Follow the manufacturer's instructions for rinsing and drying the fabric sheets.

Tip

When piecing together several fabric sheets to create one image, sew the sheets together *before* rinsing.

Construction

1. Measure the central image after piecing. Cut inner border strips $\frac{3}{4}'' \times$ the needed lengths. Sew the inner borders to the central image. Press the seam allowances toward the inner border.

2. Measure the resulting quilt top. Cut outer border strips $3\frac{1}{2}'' \times$ the needed lengths. Sew the outer borders to the inner border. Press the seam allowances toward the outer border.

3. Layer the quilt top, batting, and backing. Baste or pin to hold the layers together.

4. Machine quilt as desired, then trim the excess batting and backing.

5. Bind.

Ain't Misbehavin'

Lesley Riley, Bethesda, MD
Finished size: 19½″ × 27″

Lesley is inspired by old photos and the untold stories behind them and always includes a photo or two in her quilts. To her, a quilt is not complete without at least one. If you listen closely enough, her quilts tell a story.

This particular quilt was inspired by a photo of a mixed-media collage Lesley created a few years back. The fabrics heighten and extend the color in the photo, and the repeated photo below adds a mysterious element.

Materials

- Photo-editing software
- Inkjet transparency sheets or matte photo paper * Do not use quick drying sheets
- Golden matte medium (available at art-supply stores)
- Fat quarter white fabric for transfers
- 13″ × 21″ striped fabric for base
- Fabric scraps for contrast
- 1 yard print for backing and borders
- 1 yard paper-backed fusible web
- 1″ foam paintbrush
- 19½″ × 27″ batting
- Teflon pressing sheet

Photo Prep

1. For the larger central image, scan or open a photo in your photo-editing software. Resize it to 8″ × 10″.
2. If desired, increase the color saturation: Choose *Adjust Hue>Saturation* from *Enhance>Adjust Color*.
3. If your image includes type, choose *Image>Rotate>Flip Horizontal* to reverse or flip the image in preparation for the transfer.
4. Print the image onto an inkjet transparency sheet following the manufacturer's instructions. When you are setting the printer options, choose *Transparency* from the *Paper Type* options. *Note:* You can also print the image onto matte photo paper.
5. Use the foam paintbrush to apply the matte medium onto the white fabric. The matte medium should cover an area slightly larger than 8″ × 10″.

6. If you are using matte photo paper for the transfer, apply some of the matte medium to the image on the paper as well as to the fabric.
7. Place the transparency or matte photo paper ink side down onto the fabric. Burnish (rub) the surface with your fingers or the back of a spoon until the image is transferred. Lift a corner to make sure the image is transferring. Rub until you achieve the desired effect.
8. Remove the transparency or photo paper. Let the transfer dry, then press to soften and seal the matte medium.
9. For the repeated image, open the photo in your photo-editing software. Resize the image to the desired size. (The image in Lesley's quilt is 1″ × 1¾″.) To select the image, choose *Select>All*. The image will have a dashed outline around it. Choose *Edit>Copy* (or press Ctrl-C). In your new file, choose *Edit>Paste* (or press Ctrl-V). Copy the image as many times as desired into 2 rows of 4 images each.
10. If the image includes type, reverse it by choosing *Image>Rotate>Flip Horizontal*.
11. Repeat Steps 4–7 to print the image, apply matte medium, and transfer the image to white fabric.
12. Let the transfers dry, then press with an iron to soften and seal the medium.

Tip

If you want to reproduce Lesley's design, apply the matte medium to a 2″ × 10″ area of the fabric. Lay one row of images onto the left half of the fabric (ink side down) and burnish to transfer. Then line up the second row of images with the first row on the right side of the fabric. Burnish to transfer.

Construction

1. Apply fusible web to the back of the base collage fabrics and images. Remove the paper backing.
2. Work on the pressing sheet and use the striped fabric as a base to create a collage with the images and fabric scraps. When you are satisfied with the placement of the fabric strips and images, fuse in place on the striped base. Don't hesitate to extend strips and images beyond the base collage.
3. Stitch the collage onto the base fabric after fusing.
4. To determine how big to cut the backing fabric: Decide how big the finished quilt will be. Add the desired border width, plus an extra 1″ to go under the collaged fabric. For example, if the finished quilt is 19½″ × 27″ and the border is 3″, cut the backing fabric 23½″ × 31″.
5. Place the backing fabric right side down and center the batting on top.
6. Fold the backing to the front over the batting and top. The folded-over fabric becomes the borders.

7. Miter the corners as you would wrap a gift: Fold up each corner at a 45° angle, fold the sides toward the middle, then fold the top and bottoms in so they form a miter. Trim the excess fabric from the corners. Fuse or stitch in place.

8. Center the base fabric with the added collage onto the backing/batting.

9. Fuse the collaged quilt top onto the folded-over backing and batting.

10. Stitch the base fabric/collage through all 3 layers to quilt it.

11. To accentuate the border, stitch around the quilt ¼˝ from the outer edge. Repeat the stitching ¼˝ away from the first line.

12. Add additional quilting as desired.

Fold the corners.

Fold in the sides.

Miter the corners.

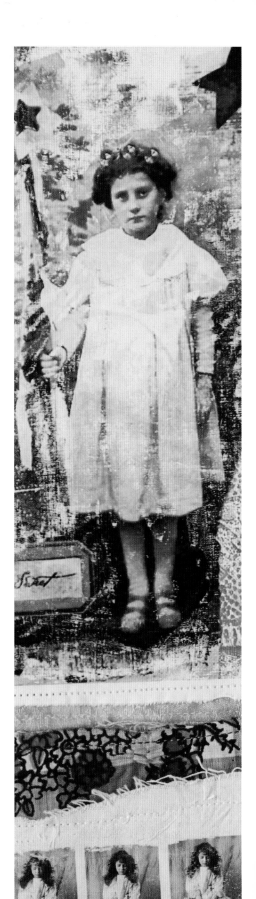

Rainbow Bars

Cyndy Lyle Rymer, Danville, CA; machine quilted by Elaine Beattie, Alamo, CA
Finished quilt size: 65$\frac{1}{2}$″ × 72$\frac{1}{2}$″

This simple design, a takeoff on the traditional Amish Bars quilt, makes it easy to incorporate both photos and reproductions of artwork. For *Rainbow Bars,* Cyndy used photographs of her fifteen-year-old daughter in addition to sketches and paintings made by her daughter. This quilt is also a great stash burner. Although Cyndy was going for subtlety in her use of photos and artwork, you can feel free to add more.

Most of the photos and drawings were scanned and then edited using the *Paint Bucket* tool in Photoshop Elements. *Paint Bucket* colorizes each image so it reads as a specific color that Cyndy could then fit in one of the vertical bars.

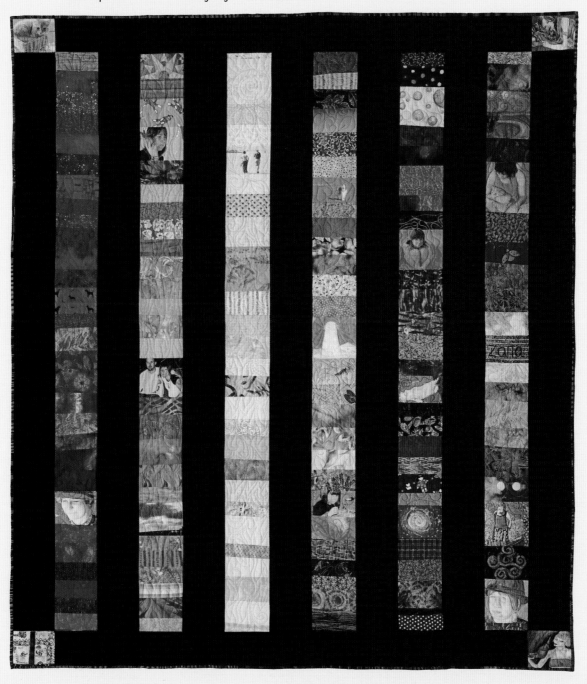

Materials

- Photo-editing software
- 6–8 pretreated 8½″ × 11″ fabric sheets, depending on how many photos or drawings you want to include in the quilt
- 3½ yards of black fabric for vertical bars and borders
- Scraps of fabric to total ⅜ yard each of red, orange, yellow, green, blue, and violet
- 3¾ yards (22″ wide) fusible interfacing for color bars
- 3⅞ yards fabric for backing
- ⅝ yard fabric for binding
- 68″ × 75″ batting

Photo Prep

1. Scan the photos and other artwork that you want to colorize (at right), and save the scans in a separate folder (label it Colorized) so they are easy to access. If you have digital photos you plan to use, place a copy of each in the new folder so that you don't accidentally modify your original photo.

2. Open the scanned images (photos and artwork) in your photo-editing software. Crop and resize the photos so each is approximately 6″ wide and varying in height from 2″ to 5½″. (See page 14 for an easy way to crop to a specific size.) If the photos aren't wide enough, add fabric strips to each side.

Tip

The scanned images are sewn onto the fusible interfacing for additional stability. The sewn strips are then trimmed to 5½″ wide. Plan for this seam allowance so you don't cut off any important features of your photos or artwork (a headless person may not be what you want).

3. Decide what color to make each photo to coordinate with your colored fabrics. Remove the color to make the image black and white (at right), then recolor (at right).

4. For instructions on printing multiple images on a page, see page 16.

Removing Color From an Image

To convert your image to black and white, choose *Enhance>Adjust Color>Remove Color.*

Colorizing a Photograph

There are many ways to recolor an image. For Photoshop Elements users, here are several you can choose from.

Paint Bucket Tool

1. Choose the *Paint Bucket* tool (see page 93).

2. To select the color you want, go down to the last icon for the *Foreground/Background* color and click on the front square. This will bring up the *Color Picker.* Choose the color you want.

3. Position the *Paint Bucket* over the area of the photo you want to change, such as the background, and click. You will probably need to reposition and repeat *Paint Bucket* several times to fill the area to your satisfaction.

Change Hue

1. Select *Enhance>Adjust Color>Adjust Hue/Saturation*

2. Use the slider bars to adjust *Hue, Saturation,* or both. Experiment with combinations of both until you get the look you want.

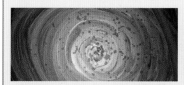

Construction

1. From each of the selected colors, cut about 25–27 pieces, each 6″ wide and varying in height from 2″ to 5½″. Trim the printed photos to this size range also. You'll need varying heights for each color bar.

2. Cut 6 strips of the fusible interfacing 6″ × 66″ for the color bars. The interfacing keeps the fabric stable as you create the long bars.

Tip

To make handling easier, cut shorter pieces of the fusible interfacing and sew in units. Then join the units together to make a 66″-long bar.

3. Starting with your red strips, pin the first piece at the top of a strip of fusible interfacing, with the rough side of the interfacing facing up. Use a dry iron to press this into position, or pin. Pin the second piece on top of the first with right sides together. Stitch, then fold the second piece down and press in place.

4. Continue stitching and flipping until the strip of fusible interfacing is covered, adding the photos and artwork randomly as you go along.

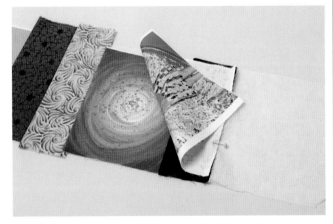

Stitch, fold, and press each successive fabric piece or printed image to the fusible interfacing.

5. Repeat for the orange, yellow, green, blue, and violet strips.

6. Trim the color bars to 5½″ × 64½″.

7. Cut 7 strips of black 5½″ × 64½″.

8. Sew the black and color bar strips together as shown in the quilt photo (page 37).

9. Cut 2 strips 4½″ × 55½″ for the top and bottom borders.

10. Sew 2 photos 5½″ × 4½″ to each end of both strips. Sew the top and bottom borders to the quilt top.

11. Layer the quilt top, batting, and backing. Baste or pin to hold the layers together.

12. Machine quilt as desired, then trim the excess batting and backing.

13. Bind.

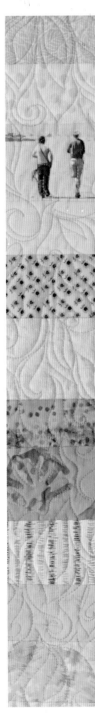
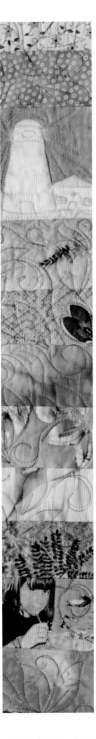

Virtual Family Reunion

Cyndy Lyle Rymer, Danville, CA
Finished panel size: 12″ × 28″

If only there were a way to make a living as a beach bum! There have been four beaches in Cyndy's life: Lavallette, New Jersey; Dennis, Massachusetts; Del Mar, California; and Pajaro Dunes, California. Her goal was to bring the memories of these special places and her favorite people together in this four-part landscape. The base for each piece is made of fast2fuse, which is also used to make some of the people pop off the surface.

Materials

- Photo-editing software
- 6–10 pretreated 8½″ × 11″ fabric sheets, depending on the number of photos to be printed
- 2 yards fast2fuse Doubled-Sided Fusible Stiff Interfacing
- Assorted fat quarters of sky blues, ocean colors, greens, and sand colors
- 1¾ yards fabric for backing
- 1 yard white tulle
- 1 yard white organza
- 1½ yards paper-backed fusible web
- Craft glue

Photo Prep

1. Scan as many photos as needed and save them using *File>New>Blank File>Preset>Letter* (see page 15). Open the photos in your photo-editing program.
2. Create a new file.
3. Use the *Move tool* (page 13) to drag the photos onto the new files as needed. Resize the photos by dragging on the corners. You will need to create more than one new file to print all of your photos.

Tip

Group the images you want to make dimensional in one or two separate files, leaving a generous ½″ between the images.

4. To kick up the color a bit before printing, choose *Enhance>Adjust Color>Adjust Hue/Saturation*. Move the slider bar to the right to the desired intensity.
5. Print each file on a pretreated fabric sheet.
6. If desired, print clouds and other landscape elements, such as flowers or dunes, on pretreated fabric sheets to use in your composition.
7. Follow the manufacturer's instructions for rinsing and drying the fabric sheets.

Construction

1. Cut apart the images you plan to mount on fast2fuse, leaving a generous ¼″ seam allowance all the way around the image.
2. Iron fusible web to the back of the rest of the images, then cut them apart.
3. Cut 4 panels of fast2fuse 12″ × 28″.
4. Cut 4 rectangles of backing fabric 14″ × 30″. Fuse the backing fabric to each fast2fuse panel. Trim the excess backing fabric even with the fast2fuse.
5. Cut strips of fabric from the sky, ocean, sand, and dune or grass colors in random widths, making sure they are at least 15″ wide. Start from the top and work down, pinning the strips on the fast2fuse panels. Make sure the strips overlap by at least ½″ on the top and bottom of each strip so the fast2fuse does not show through. If desired, occasionally insert strips of printed landscape elements.
6. Work on one panel at a time to fuse the fabric strips to the fast2fuse.
7. Trim the edges of the strips so they are straight. Wrap the fabric to the back of the covered fast2fuse and use craft glue to adhere the fabric to the back.
8. Quilt along the edges of each panel.
9. Fuse the photos you have chosen to be dimensional to scraps of fast2fuse. Wrap the seam allowance to the back and glue in place, clipping curves as necessary.
10. Position the photos on each panel. Consider placing some photos under a layer of organza or tulle to add another dimensional quality to the panel.
11. When you are satisfied with the placement of all of your photos, fuse them in place. Use a bit of glue on the back of the dimensional photos.

Clover Lake

Joyce R. Becker, Kent, WA, 2006
Finished quilt size: 30″ × 23″

This quilt was created in response to Joyce's personal challenge to make a poster-size landscape quilt from a digital photograph. Once the original photograph was printed onto pretreated fabric sheets, Joyce's goal was to camouflage the joining lines so they were not apparent.

Joyce says, "By putting on my problem-solving hat, I accomplished my objective by cutting the joined edges in curvy lines. I replaced the printed sky with commercial fabric, adding fabric trees and rocks in the foreground to mask the lines. Overlays of bonded Angelina helped disguise the joining lines in the water. For added texture and dimension, I enhanced some of the trees and the mountains with extensive machine embroidery and added three-dimensional foliage shapes."

Original photo   Photo by Dan Neil

Materials

- Photo-editing software
- 12–15 pretreated 8½″ × 11″ fabric sheets
- 37″ × 30″ muslin for the base
- 37″ × 30″ lightweight fusible interfacing
- ½ yard blue fabric to match sky in photograph
- ½ yard green fabric for trees
- ¼ yard gray-brown fabric for boulders
- ¼ yard yellow-orange fabric for foliage
- 1½ yards fabric for backing and binding
- 32″ × 25″ batting
- ½ yard paper-backed fusible web (optional)
- Angelina fibers: Crystal Aurora Borealis, Peacock Green, Opal Sparkle (see Resources on page 94)
- Gray and brown Tsukineko Fabrico Fabric Markers (see Resources on page 94)
- 505 Spray and Fix adhesive
- Invisible thread
- Bo-Nash 007 Bonding Agent (see Resources on page 94)
- Teflon pressing sheet

Photo Prep

1. Open the photo in your photo-editing software.
2. Adjust the color saturation, brightness, contrast, and hue as necessary. Make any other adjustments to your photo as needed.
3. Decide on the final size of your quilt. Joyce used 15 sheets, but you can make your quilt any size you like.

Tip

Create a test print using plain copy paper in *Poster mode* (see pages 9–10). Use the *Fast Draft* option under *Copy Quality* to save ink. The test print shows you how your photo will be divided.

If your printer does not offer poster printing, you can manually divide and enlarge your photo in sections (see pages 18–19 and 30) or you can use a service.

4. When you are satisfied with your composition, print on the pretreated fabric sheets.
5. Follow the manufacturer's instructions for rinsing and drying the fabric sheets.

Construction

1. Iron fusible interfacing on top of the muslin base and put it up on a design wall.
2. Assemble the printed landscape, starting with the bottom right corner. Pin the first block in your photograph onto the muslin. Turn under and press the white margin on the top edge.
3. Position and pin the next block in your photograph in order. Turn under and press the margin on the right and top edges.

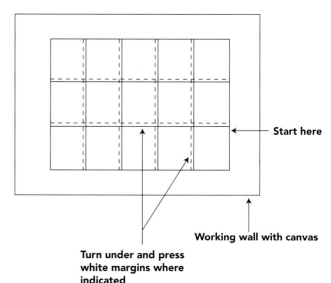

Start here

Working wall with canvas

Turn under and press white margins where indicated

4. Continue building rows in order, turning and pressing the margins as indicated until your image is complete.

5. Take down each piece and one by one cut a *very* narrow (not even ¼˝ wide), gentle curvy line only on the pressed edges. This trims away the white margin and leaves a curvy edge to overlap the adjacent sheets.

Tip

When you view a landscape, your eye auto-matically goes to straight lines. If you cut your lines curvy, they will be less apparent. After the quilt is put together, layers of tulle, Angelina fibers, landscaping elements such as trees or flowers, and finally lots of quilting will help disguise the areas where the separate sections of the photo were joined.

Cut curvy lines on the pressed edges.

6. Working in order, from bottom right to left, assemble the trimmed, printed photos on your stabilized muslin canvas, overlapping the cut edges. Glue all but the top row in place with the 505 Spray and Fix adhesive.

7. Before gluing the top row in place, cut away the printed sky and the top margin on each block.

8. Press, cut, position, and glue the sky fabric behind the top row of blocks.

9. Now you can place the top row of blocks—right to left—onto the canvas, overlapping the cut edges, and glue in place.

10. Cut out trees and boulders from the fabrics. Position and glue them in place.

11. Cut out shapes to resemble foliage, and glue them into place. *Optional:* For added dimension, use fusible web to join 2 layers of matching foliage fabrics with the wrong sides together.

12. Machine baste the design with invisible thread and matching lightweight bobbin thread.

13. Shade boulders with fabric markers, if desired.

14. With matching threads, free-motion machine embroider the crevices and outline of the mountains,

the trees in the distance, and the large fir tree boughs. One of the reasons Joyce's quilt is so beautiful is the embroidery and quilting she added.

15. Follow the manufacturer's instructions, and use a low-temperature iron to create individual pieces of the Angelina fibers for overlays in the water.

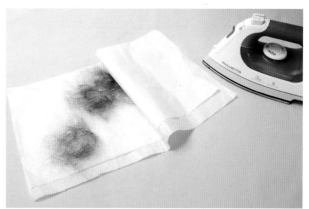

Fuse Angelina fibers between sheets of tissue paper.

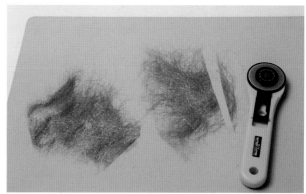

Bonded fibers are ready to be cut up.

16. Bond the Angelina overlays into place on your design with Bo-Nash 007 Bonding Agent, following the manufacturer's instructions.

17. Layer the quilt top, batting, and backing. Baste or pin to hold the layers together.

18. Machine quilt as desired, then trim the excess batting and backing.

19. Bind.

Falling Leaves

Cyndy Lyle Rymer, Danville, CA
Finished quilt size: 35″ × 27″

Here's a different approach to using a large poster-printed image cut into smaller pieces. The sky in Cyndy's printed photos was a bit dull, so she decided to add a painted overlay of organza to boost the colors. Additional texture was added when the piece was quilted and the organza was cut away to reveal parts of the image underneath, as inspired by Danish quilt artist Charlotte Yde.

Materials

- Photo-editing software
- 6 pretreated $8\frac{1}{2}" \times 11"$ fabric sheets (regular or fusible)
- $2\frac{1}{2}$ yards black fabric for background, backing, and binding
- 1 yard organza
- Marking pencil
- Fabric or acrylic paints
- 1" foam paintbrush
- Fall leaves
- Sharp-tipped embroidery scissors
- Pressing cloth
- 1 yard paper-backed fusible web
- $37" \times 29"$ batting
- *Optional:* Large rubber stamps of leaves

Photo Prep

1. Open the photo in your photo-editing software.
2. Print the image in poster mode 2 pages wide x 2 pages high (see pages 18–19) using regular or fusible pretreated fabric sheets.
3. Place fall leaves on your all-in-one scanner bed and copy onto fabric.
4. Follow the manufacturer's instructions for rinsing and drying the fabric sheets.

Construction

1. For the photo, if you aren't using fusible pretreated fabric sheets, iron fusible web to the back of each printed fabric sheet. Trim any excess white areas and then cut each printed sheet into pieces approximately $1\frac{1}{4}" \times 1\frac{1}{4}"$. Trim away any unprinted areas.
2. From the black fabric, cut a rectangle $37" \times 29"$ for the background. Fold it in quarters to create guidelines. Use the marking pencil to draw horizontal lines $1\frac{1}{2}"$ apart.
3. Start at the top left corner and work across each guideline, carefully positioning each cut piece so the base aligns with a marked guideline.

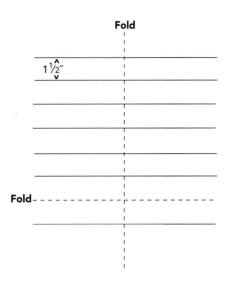

Sketch out the grid on the background.

4. When all the pieces are in position, fuse them in place.
5. Place the organza on a piece of plastic to protect your work surface. Thin down acrylic or textile paints with a bit of water, then paint the organza in wide bands of color to enhance your photo. Allow the fabric to dry.
6. Position the organza on top of the fused pieces.
7. Layer the quilt top, batting, and backing. Baste or pin to hold the layers together.
8. Quilt in a grid between and outside the fused pieces.
9. Very carefully pierce random sections of the organza with the tip of your scissors and cut it away to reveal the printed photo below.
10. For the copied images of fall leaves, if you aren't using fusible pretreated fabric sheets, iron fusible web to the back of the printed fabric sheet, cut out the leaves, and fuse them onto your quilt top.
11. To add more depth, stamp leaf images onto the quilt. Use a foam brush to lightly coat your rubber stamp with paint or ink, then stamp.
12. Outline quilt the printed and stamped leaves and then quilt additional leaves. Trim the excess batting and backing.
13. Bind.

Gramsie

Jeanie Sumrall-Ajero, Fort Collins, CO

Finished size: 35″ × 36½″

A few years ago, Jeanie and her mother were sorting through old family photos, and Jeanie was struck by how much fun her grandmother had had in her younger years. A picture of her grandmother by the seaside in California with her head thrown back laughing is Jeanie's absolute favorite. Taking a cue from the playfulness of the photo, Jeanie turned the photo into a kaleidoscope to use as the focal point of a quilt. Additional photos of her grandmother at various ages complete this tribute to her Gramsie.

Materials

Kaleidoscope Collections Kaleidoscope Kreator 2.0 software (see Resources on page 94)
Photo-editing software

- 6 pretreated $8\frac{1}{2}'' \times 11''$ fabric sheets
- $\frac{1}{4}$ yard dark blue fabric for narrow borders
- $\frac{1}{4}$ yard medium blue fabric for borders
- $\frac{1}{8}$ yard light blue fabric for narrow photo borders
- $\frac{1}{4}$ yard tan fabric for setting triangles
- $\frac{1}{4}$ yard brown fabric for narrow inner border
- $\frac{3}{4}$ yard fabric for outer border and binding
- $1\frac{1}{4}$ yards fabric for backing
- $\frac{1}{4}''$-wide Steam-A-Seam 2 fusible hem tape
- $1\frac{1}{8}$ yards beaded fringe (optional)
- $37'' \times 39''$ batting

Photo Prep

1. Scan the photos if they are not already in digital format. If you are scanning old and faded photos, use the scanner's auto-correction features to darken the photos and to increase the contrast.

Tip

If the photos are smaller than 4″, set the scanner resolution to 600 dpi so you will be able to enlarge them without sacrificing quality. Save each photo to its own file.

2. Open each of the coordinating photos in your photo-editing program. Crop each photo to 4.1″ x 4.1″ at 300 dpi (see page 14).

Before and after cropping

3. To add a seam allowance around the photo, choose *Image>Resize>Canvas Size,* and set the height and width to 4.5″. Make sure the center anchor point is set (this is the default). Click on the little color block at the bottom of the dialog box for the canvas extension color and set the color to light gray. Click *OK.* You will use the edge of the canvas as a cutting guide.

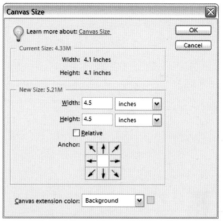

Create an additional seam allowance by enlarging the canvas size.

4. To create a sepia tone for the coordinating photos, choose *Enhance>Adjust Color>Adjust Hue/Saturation.* Check the box for *Colorize* (at the bottom of the screen), which will automatically set *Hue* to 240 and *Saturation* to 25. Enter 35 for *Hue* to change the tone of the photo from gray to sepia.

5. Print 2 photos per sheet of pretreated fabric.

6. Launch Kaleidoscope Kreator 2.0 and open the digital photo for the center of the quilt. Select the *Square (08)* template shape and position the photo in the template to create a kaleidoscope to your liking.

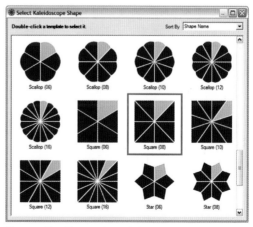

Choose the *Square* template.

7. Click on the *Preview Kaleidoscope* button to view a full-screen preview of your kaleidoscope. (Refer to the *Help file* or the Quick Start Video Tutorial on the product CD if you need help positioning your photo.)

8. If the subject of the photo doesn't fill the template shape, make a note of where the photo needs to be extended. Exit Kaleidoscope Kreator and edit the photo in your photo-editing software. Use the *Clone Stamp tool* (see below) to extend just the portion of the photo you need to fill the template shape. To combine any layers in the edited photo, choose *Layer>Flatten Image*. Save your edited photo to a new file, then open in Kaleidoscope Kreator and reposition.

Clone Stamp Tool

The *Clone Stamp tool* takes a sample of the pixels in an area of your photo so you can "paint over" parts of the photo that you don't want (for example, a pole that is sticking out of a person's head) or, as in this case, extend the photo a bit.

Select the *Clone Stamp tool*.

Place the pointer on the area you want to use and Alt-click (hold the Alt key on your keyboard and click with your mouse at the same time). You will now "paint" with that color by dragging with the tool. Select the brush style and size from the options bar.

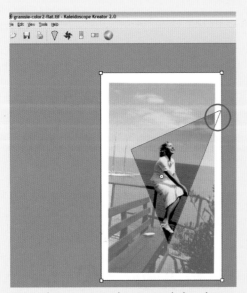

Note where you need to extend the photo.

9. Choose *File>Save Workspace* to save the position of your photo in the template shape so that you can recreate the kaleidoscope if needed.

10. When you are pleased with your kaleidoscope design, print it using Kaleidoscope Kreator's *Print Poster* feature (*File>Custom Print Options>Print Poster*). Specify a 2 × 2 (4) arrangement to create 8˝ tiles (printed fabric sections). If your printer has a ⅛˝ print margin (rather than a ¼˝ print margin), you will also need to specify a 0.10˝ print margin to get a good ¼˝ seam allowance around the tile.

Increase the margin size before printing.

Note: Practice printing on paper first in *Draft* mode to save ink. Then print on the pretreated fabric sheets.

11. Follow the manufacturer's instructions for rinsing and drying the fabric sheets for the additional photos. *Do not rinse the poster-printed sheets yet.*

Construction

1. Use a ruler and rotary cutter to trim away the excess white fabric from the sepia-tone photos. The photos (including the extra "canvas" that was added in Photo Prep Steps 2 and 3) should be 4½˝ × 4½˝.

2. Use a ruler and rotary cutter to trim the kaleidoscope tiles. *Leave ¼˝ of white fabric around the edge of each tile.*

3. Cut the following strips the width of the fabric:
   - Dark blue (A): Cut 2 strips $1\frac{1}{4}''$ wide and 3 strips $1''$ wide.
   - Medium blue (B): Cut 2 strips $1\frac{3}{4}''$ wide and 3 strips $1''$ wide.
   - Light blue (C): Cut 3 strips $1''$ wide.
   - Tan (D): Cut 4 squares $7\frac{7}{8}'' \times 7\frac{7}{8}''$, then cut diagonally to create triangles.
   - Brown (E): Cut 4 strips $1''$ wide.
   - Borders and binding (F): Cut 4 strips $3\frac{1}{2}''$ wide for the border and 4 strips $2\frac{1}{2}''$ wide for the binding.

4. Sew together the tiles (printed sections) to make the kaleidoscope, *then* rinse by following the manufacturer's instructions.

5. Sew the top and bottom tiles together first, pressing the seams in opposite directions. Then sew the top half to the bottom half. The easiest way to match the images along the seams is to first press back $\frac{1}{4}''$ of one of the tiles along the seam line. Apply a strip of the $\frac{1}{4}''$ Steam-A-Seam 2 to the folded seam allowance. Line up the 2 tiles and press together, then open the folded tile and stitch down the crease. Repeat for all seams in the kaleidoscope.

6. Sew the $1\frac{1}{4}''$ A strips around the outside of the kaleidoscope. Trim away the tails.

7. Sew the $1\frac{3}{4}''$ B strips around the outside of A. Trim the tails.

8. Use each $4\frac{1}{2}'' \times 4\frac{1}{2}''$ photo as the center square of a Log Cabin block. Sew $1''$ C strips to the sides of each photo. Cut apart and sew the remaining $1''$ C strips to the tops and bottoms of the photos. Repeat with the $1''$ B strips and then the $1''$ A strips to create four $7\frac{1}{2}'' \times 7\frac{1}{2}''$ blocks.

9. Sew the short edges of the D triangles to adjacent sides of the Log Cabin blocks you just created. (You may want to lay out the pieces on the table to make sure they are oriented correctly.) Trim if necessary.

10. Sew the resulting triangles to the kaleidoscope piece. Trim if necessary.

11. Sew the $1''$ E strips around the outer edge.

12. Sew the $3\frac{1}{2}''$ F strips around the outer edge.

13. Layer the quilt top, batting, and backing. Baste or pin to hold the layers together.

14. Machine quilt as desired, then trim the excess batting and backing.

15. Bind.

16. *Optional:* Sew beaded fringe along the bottom edge of the quilt.

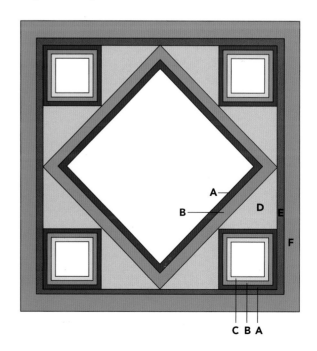

Empty Nest

Alethea Ballard, Walnut Creek, CA
Finished quilt size: 50″ × 39″

A couple of years ago, Alethea began buying and potting succulent plants. Soon, dozens of these unusual plants were spilling across her yard, and her obsession with the plants grew. Looking back, Alethea realizes that the plants provided a way to "feather her empty nest."

Materials

- Photo-editing software
- 9 pretreated 8½″ × 11″ fabric sheets
- ⅛ yard each or scraps of colors in your images (in this case, greens, pinks, grays, and blues)
- ⅛ yard each of 8 assorted prints for borders
- 1½ yards fabric for backing
- ⅜ yard fabric for binding
- ⅔ yard paper-backed fusible web
- 52″ × 41″ batting

Photo Prep

1. Open your main image in your photo-editing program. Choose *Enhance>Adjust Color>Adjust Hue/Saturation* and then move the slider bar to the right to the desired intensity.
2. Divide the central image into 4 quarters (see page 18). Print on 4 pretreated fabric sheets.
3. Choose 14 images and resize them so they are all 4″ × 6″ (see page 14).
4. Print the photos on pretreated fabric sheets, arranging them in groups of 3 per fabric sheet (page 16).
5. Follow the manufacturer's instructions for rinsing and drying the fabric sheets.

Construction

1. Cut a variety of fabric scraps into 4½″ × 2¼″ rectangles. Stack them, right sides up, and then cut along the diagonal, using a slight curve if you wish.
2. Stitch pairs together. Sew the stitched pairs into long strips. Trim the strips to 1¾″ × the desired length.

Faux Pieced Sashing

Replace the pieced sashing with a striped fabric to achieve a similar look simply and quickly.

3. Place the printed photos on a design board or wall and audition the fabric strips (refer to the project photo for placement).
4. Select scraps to use for the abstract leaf patterns. Iron fusible web to the back of the fabrics, trace the abstract leaf patterns (see page 54) on the right side, and cut out. Fuse the leaf shapes to 24 rectangles

3½″ × 2¼″ and 14 rectangles 4½″ × 2¼″. Arrange these on the design wall.

5. When you are pleased with the arrangement, sew the photos and leaf blocks into vertical rows, trimming the leaf blocks as needed to fit. Add the pieced strips.
6. Sew pieced strips between the 4 central photos to create a large block, then add the leaf blocks and pieced strips above and below the central square. Add the remaining photo and leaf blocks, trimming as needed to fit.
7. For the borders, position 3½″ strips right sides up so that they overlap by about 2″ in the center. Cut along the length in an S curve. Flip one on top of the other and pin, then sew using a scant ¼″ seam. Repeat for the other borders. Clip the seams as needed. Press.

8. Add the borders to the quilt top.
9. Square the quilt top.
10. Layer the quilt top, batting, and backing. Baste or pin to hold the layers together.
11. Quilt. Alethea quilted long, curvy lines across the pieced sections. The photos were not quilted, but Alethea anchored the images with small stitches. Trim the excess batting and backing.
12. Bind.

Patterns for leaf blocks

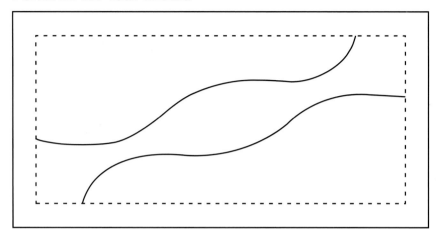

For 4½″ x 2¼″ Rectangle

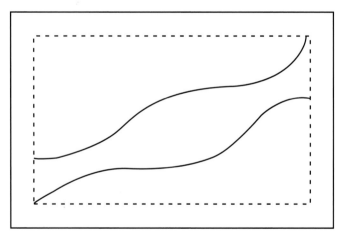

For 3½″ x 2¼″ Rectangle

Chic Music

Cyndy Lyle Rymer, Danville, CA
Finished quilt size: each panel 12″ × 13″

Pick a theme and use it to experiment with any and all techniques. Cyndy's inspirations for *Chic Music* were the lyrics of songs recorded by some of her favorite female artists. It's easy to find the lyrics on the Internet. Cyndy says she doesn't ever want to finish—so many great songs, so little time. Photoshop Elements provideds a wonderful variety of ways to alter the personal original photos as well as those that Cyndy found on collage sheets, which are collections of vintage images usually grouped by theme.

For *Chic Music*, Cyndy created 12 panels, each interpreting a favorite song. The other panels are shown in the Gallery on pages 72–73.

Supremes "Stop in the Name of Love"

This was the first song Cyndy interpreted because she has always loved the Supremes. On the left, Cyndy used *Layer* (page 18) to merge a photo of a door with a photo of a stop sign. A photo of her daughter converted from color to black and white (see page 38) was repeated on the right. Lonni Rossi fabrics provided the perfect accompaniment. The word "love" was quilted in red in a variety of languages in the middle of the little quilt.

k.d. lang "Miss Chatelaine"

An image of a medieval damsel transferred from a photo printed on matte photo paper (see page 35) is layered with an inkjet print of the same image. Locks and keys printed on ExtravOrganza appear in the background, and found objects were added. A piece of organza ribbon trimmed with tiny pearls was the perfect background for the medieval-style purple border at left and on the bottom.

Madeleine Peyroux "You're Gonna Make Me Lonesome When You Go"

This rendition of the Bob Dylan tune inspired Cyndy to use *Layer* (page 18) for the image on the right. A photo of a river scene provided the base, a different photo of large clouds was merged with it, and finally the figure of a man fades into the top right corner. On the left, a thermofax of an open door was printed on white fabric with fabric paint, then a photo of a lonely woman and flowers against a white picket fence was printed on ExtravOrganza and fused on top of the door. Scraps of hand-dyed fabrics were added to complete the piece.

Materials

The materials you use will depend on how you choose to interpret your theme and how many panels you choose to make. Suggested supplies are as follows.

- Photo-editing software
- 8–10 pretreated fabric sheets (regular or fusible)
- 3 sheets Jacquard ExtravOrganza
- Fat quarters or large scraps of fabrics for backgrounds
- 2½ yards black sateen for backing, borders, and binding
- Scraps of fabrics to fit the themes
- 13˝ × 14˝ pieces of batting
- Angelina fibers
- Collage sheets (see Resources on page 94)
- Organza
- Fabric paints and foam paintbrushes
- Freezer paper
- Rubber stamps and inkpads
- Gluestick
- Fusible web
- Yarns and other fibers for embellishing
- Found objects, such as keys, chains, etc.
- Crop-a-Dile or other hole punch to make holes for eyelets to string the panels together
- Black eyelets and key chains

Photo Prep

1. If you plan to use images from collage sheets, scan the sheets. Open the files of your collages in your photo-editing program and save the appropriate images in separate files.
2. Open photos and just start playing with the different *Filter* options (see page 17). Save a few options in separate files until you know what you want to do.
3. Group the images in a new blank file (see page 16) and print on pretreated fabric sheets.
4. Back the images with fusible web if you aren't using fusible pretreated fabric sheets.

Construction

1. Cut each background piece about 13˝ × 14˝. These will be trimmed later.
2. Arrange the fusible-backed printed photos and other objects on your background fabrics, which can be any fabrics you choose to use—black sateen, commercial fabrics, hand-dyed fabrics, and so on.
3. Fuse or stitch the photos onto the background fabrics.
4. Quilt each piece. Echo quilting is almost always a great choice. Trim each piece to 12˝ × 13˝.
5. Cut 2˝ strips of fabric. Bind each panel separately.
6. Just to get you started, here are a few of the techniques Cyndy used:

Connecting the panels

Cyndy punched holes, inserted eyelets, and connected her panels with beaded chain. You could also use large safety pins, ribbon, or extensions of the side bindings.

Galleries

According to a fall 2006 article in *Surface Design Journal,* people have been printing photos on fabrics since the early 1800s, using a wide variety of methods. Thanks to digital cameras and inkjet printers—and photo-editing programs such as Photoshop—the process has become accessible to a wider variety of quilters and other artists. Digital printing on fabric has become another vehicle for jumping the boundaries of traditional quiltmaking.

It's all about surface design, and the galleries that follow showcase artists who are exploring the possibilities. The subject matter varies widely: Ordinary objects such as flowers, locks and hinges, or the landscape surveyed during daily walks, are manipulated and transformed into images that take them beyond the ordinary. Original works of art such as paintings, hand-dyed fabric, or quilts are used as the basis for creating second-generation pieces of new art. Personal expression is taken to new heights with creative approaches and techniques.

Royal Crustacean, Rose Rushbrooke, Aldie, VA, 14″ × 16″

This quilt took shape from an original fractal computer design that Rose says resembles a purple-colored lobster, a color used by royalty for their garments. Silk charmeuse was prepared with Bubble Jet Set 2000. The piece was hand embroidered with French knots made with silk ribbon and hand quilted with hand-dyed cotton thread. The edges were frayed, and then the piece was mounted on stretched canvas painted silver.

Going in Circles I, Gloria Hansen,
Hightstown, NJ, 47″ × 47″

Gloria is one of the original digital artists and a master at her craft. For this quilt, she created an original design
in Adobe Illustrator, then manipulated it in Photoshop. The design was printed onto cotton fabric with archival
inks. D'UVA pastels enhance the original images on fabric.

Sun and Stars Goes Super-Nova, Lynn Koolish, Berkeley, CA, 24″ × 24″

The original image for this quilt was another quilt made by the artist. Lynn manipulated a digital photo of the quilt in Photoshop, using the *Twirl* and *Wave* filters until she decided the new image stood on its own as a new work. Lynn says, "When manipulating images in Photoshop, I love the challenge of working with the surprise I get when trying new filters and effects, and then manipulating them to create dynamic new images."

Doll Face, Elin Waterston, South Salem, NY, 12″ × 12″

The central image was created from a direct scan of a plastic doll face purchased at a craft-supply store. Elin used Photoshop to intensify the contrast and brightness of the image, which she then printed onto a pretreated fabric sheet. To make the fabric that surrounds the doll image, she printed text onto a piece of red cotton fabric treated with Bubble Jet Set 2000. This quilt was then machine pieced and machine quilted, and finally hand couched and embellished with glass beads, trim, and plastic baby dolls.

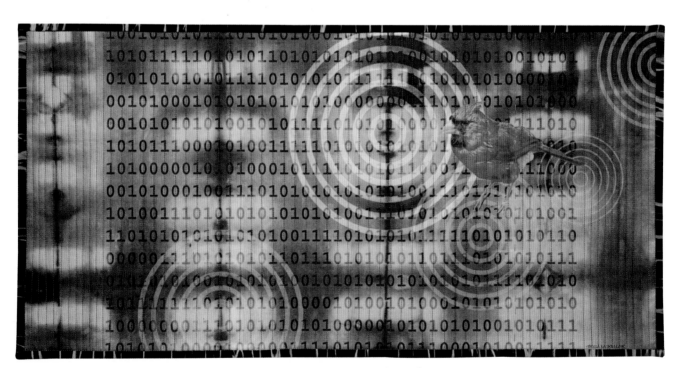

Bird in Digital Shibori Landscape, Tricia McKellar, Fuquay-Varina, NC, 36″ × 18″

Tricia digitally altered photographs of her own hand-dyed shibori fabrics in Photoshop, which is also where she often slips in other images during the process—such as the photo of a cardinal. She printed the digital collage on silk using Lyson Cave Paint pigment inks. Tricia usually machine quilts her pieces, sometimes adding hand quilting for texture.

Dangling Participles, Lonni Rossi,
Wynnewood, PA, 35³/₄″ × 35³/₄″

This quilt was made for Dancing Between the
Semicolons: An Exhibit In and Of the Cloth. Found
objects, flowers, leaves, pods, or seeds are often the
inspiration for Lonni's artwork. After scanning these
objects, she used Adobe Freehand, Illustrator, and
Photoshop to manipulate them into patterns, often
using QuarkXPress or Freehand to add bits of text,
handwriting, and so forth. She used film positives to
make photographic silk screens for printing on fabrics
such as cotton, linen, canvas, silk, or rayon. Hand
painting and embroidery added to the surface design.

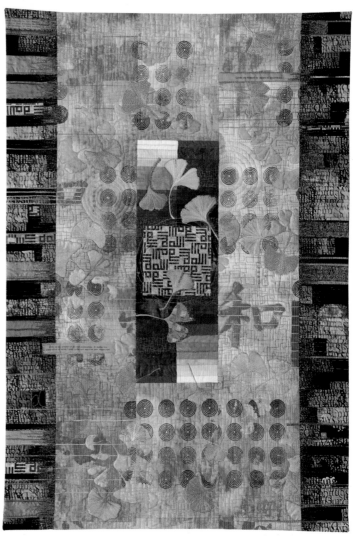

Harmony, Lonni Rossi, Wynnewood, PA, 30″ × 43¹/₄″

This symbolic and beautiful quilt was made to
honor the 50th birthday of Lonni's sister, Netti.
Five ginkgo leaves in the center celebrate each
decade, and personal messages of praise and
encouragement decorate the hand-painted fabric,
as well as the fabrics created with silk-screened
images and laser printing. The Sufi type in the
center was created in Adobe Freehand.

Grotto, Diane Rusin Doran, Glenelg, MD, 42″ × 53″

A multitalented artist, Diane scanned fragments of her original painting, then manipulated and collaged them using Corel PHOTO-PAINT and CorelDRAW. She printed them on fabric, did extensive quilting by machine, and used colored pencils to enhance parts of the design.

Grotto, Diane Rusin Doran, Glenelg, MD, 42″ × 53″

Fun With Finger Paints, Jeanie Sumrall-Ajero, Fort Collins, CO, 52″ × 68″

The innovator responsible for Kaleidoscope Kreator 2 software says she is always on the lookout for different images she can use. She loves to combine the new with the traditional—in this case, computer-generated kaleidoscope designs featured in a traditional quilt pattern. Looking for a different feeling than photographs would provide, Jeanie was inspired by her young nephew to try finger painting for the first time in decades. She focused on the blend of colors and swirls to create a painting that served as a stepping-stone to making more-intricate kaleidoscope designs with Kaleidoscope Kreator software. After searching for a quilt block that would showcase her custom-designed fabrics, Jeanie used the Royal Gems pattern by Toby Lischko, published by Make It Easy.

Quilt photo by
Barbara McKie

Surface Departure #2, Barbara Barrick McKie, Lyme, CT, 25″ × 25″

As her starting point, Barbara used her original silk shibori designs, created with silk dyes and a pleater. She scanned and manipulated the designs in Photoshop 6, then printed them on polyester crepe using disperse dyes. After appliquéing them onto black Pimatex cotton, she mounted the three-dimensional pieces on the background pieces. Barbara used a stiffener to keep the shapes dimensional. Extensive quilting embellishes the work.

Rust and Wood, Nancy Herman, Merion, PA, 20″ × 68″

Nancy enjoys exploring her immediate environment with the help of her camera's zoom lens, which allows her to play with the images' innate symmetry to create new textures. With Photoshop, she manipulated shots of old locks and hinges found on wood and decorated with moss, and then had the image printed onto fabric by Silicon Gallery. Nancy states that she would "like to create gardens of my own out of old shoes and broken glass through the magic of modern technology."

Quilt image provided by Lura Schwarz Smith

Off the Plate and Off With the Drape, Lura Schwarz Smith, Coarsegold, CA, 23″ × 28″

Lura and husband, Kerby, teamed up to create this combination of one of Lura's original drawings (which Kerby photographed) and Kerby's digital images. After printing the images on pretreated fabric, Lura used her favorite Tsukineko inks and textile markers to enhance them. The quilt, which was inspired by the classic nudes depicted in Italian artwork that the couple saw on a trip to Tuscany, was fused and machine appliquéd.

I'm Not at This Address, Cindy McNutt-Kaestner, Philomath, OR, 49″ × 37″

Seventy years' worth of photos celebrate a life well lived, while the making of this quilt helped Cindy deal with the grief she experienced when her mom, Audaleen Hollis Harris McNutt, passed away. Cindy's husband, Richard, scanned the photos, then Cindy used Microsoft Office Picture Manager to make adjustments. The background rectangles were pieced and quilted at the same time with clear thread. Then the entire quilt was quilted again and cut and burned with a burning tool. After printing the photos on pretreated fabric, Cindy added the photo montage to the quilt. Cindy then sewed the piece with thick leather cording, cut the quilt again, and folded it in three places to form a heart-shaped quilt. Embellishments include her mom's trinkets and old jewelry.

Facing the Past, Marion Coleman, Castro Valley, CA, 13½″ × 13½″

A high-contrast photo printed in red provides an effective background for family photos that Marion scanned and printed using Photoshop Elements. She transferred other photos onto solid and printed fabrics. Marion then fused and quilted the quilt with a variety of threads, with words depicting Marion's role in life scattered throughout.

Brittle Silence, Linda Colsh, Everberg, Belgium, 33″ × 38″

Linda created the image of "the Omega woman reprised in her isolation: in the dark, invisible" from a photo using Photoshop. She discharged and printed her images on cotton fabric, then machine pieced and quilted.

Quilt photo by Pol Leemans, Fotostudio Leemans

Dressing Up, Sandi Cummings, Moraga, CA, 55″ × 71″

Dressing Up is a quilt that Sandi created from an original photograph. Although she was making a quilt *about* children, she didn't want it to be a children's quilt, so Sandi tried to keep the design elements fairly sophisticated and the fabric selection light and airy. She sewed colored netting over the printed hats for added color, while retaining the combination of light and shadow reflected on the hats in the photograph. The faces on the quilt were printed on cotton broadcloth by Joolia Harper on an Epson 9600, which will print images up to 44″ wide.

Shadow, Wen Redmond, Strafford, NH, 18″ × 21″

An image taken on Deer Isle, Massachusetts, was copied and divided into nine separate images. Wen printed the images twice—once on transparent silk organza and a second time on background sewing stabilizer. She sewed the images together and added borders of hand-dyed, hand-painted, and silk-screened fabrics. The piece was mounted on a stretcher bar frame.

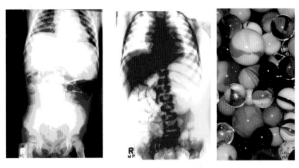

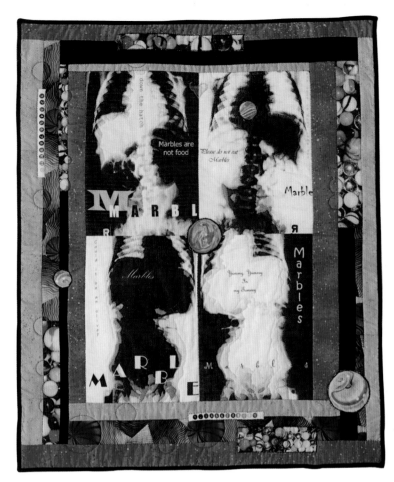

Marble Run, Karylee Doubiago, Adams, MA, 22″ × 27″

Here's a frightening experience turned into a humorous piece of art. Karylee re-photographed the X-rays of the marbles lodged inside her three-year-old twins' tummies and photographed the actual marbles "involved in the incident." The photos of the marbles were used as an accent fabric. Before printing the images on pretreated fabric, Karylee added the words. Karylee is happy to report that "neither the children nor the marbles were harmed in the making of this quilt."

Magic Is Everywhere, Lesley Riley, Bethesda, MD, 17¹/₂″ × 25″

As silent records of the past, photographs are integral to Lesley's work. For this quilt, she chose a nineteenth-century hand-tinted tintype and increased the saturation of the image in Photoshop. She then transferred the image to white fabric using matte medium. The buttons are derived from a vintage bird print that Lesley reduced, printed on an inkjet printer, and used to cover buttons.

Chic Music, Cyndy Lyle Rymer, Danville, CA, 12″ × 13″ each

Bonnie Raitt "No Getting Over You"

A tie-dyed blue-and-white fabric is the base for a variety of images that conjure up the lyrics from one song by an all-time favorite musician.

Judy Collins "Who Knows Where the Time Goes"

A sunset photo is layered with clock images printed on ExtravOrganza, then bordered with purple shibori-dyed fabric. The organza was trimmed in places to reveal the image beneath.

Basia "Copernicus"

Photoshop Elements *Layers* was a great vehicle for creating a collage of images. Some of the images were printed on ExtravOrganza for a translucent look.

Sade "Kiss of Life"

A dogwood blossom, an angel from a collage sheet by Picture Trails/Lost Art Creations, and a heart were printed separately on ExtravOrganza, then stitched to one incredibly bright fabric background.

Jonatha Brooke "The Story, So Much Mine"

As the mother of a teenage girl, Cyndy gets shivers up her spine when she hears this song. Her husband's eyes and her hands sewing were naturals to illustrate the lyrics. A thermo-faxed image (screen provided by quilt artist Sandi Cummings) was screened large, then scanned, repeated, and reduced for the smaller image at the bottom. The smaller dress was made with fast2fuse and painted fabric.

Joni Mitchell "A Case of You"

Cyndy's favorite song of all time. A photo of a case of wine was adjusted using *Filter>Distort>Ocean Ripple*. Using *Layer*, Cyndy added a traced map of Canada and turned down the *Opacity* a few notches. The photo of a watercolor-paint box was enlarged and the color saturated. After the photos were printed, she applied fusible web to the back, cut up the photos, and then fused it all to a black background.

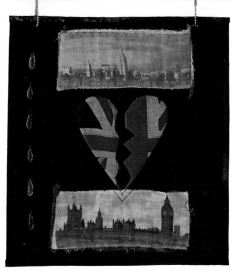

Corinne Bailey Rae "Butterfly"

A wonderful song about finding your wings. The lyrics called for a photo of the house Cyndy grew up in, a framed photo of herself as a young girl, and lots of butterflies. The butterflies—and butterfly wings—are from a collage sheet by Picture Trails/Lost Art Creations that was printed on ExtravOrganza.

Melissa Etheridge "Bring Me Some Water"

After seeing Melissa Etheridge in concert one summer, Cyndy had to do this song. The flames are a photo of a fire in her grill; the girl is from a collage sheet.

Julia Fordham "Manhattan Skyline"

A favorite song of Cyndy's from the 1980s depicts the heart rending pain of trying to maintain a long-distance relationship.

See page 55 for the fourth set of panels.

Newspaper images used with permission of Boulder Daily Camera

Elegy, Carol Watkins, Boulder, CO, 22″ × 30″

This piece, which reflects Carol's ongoing concern about the war in Iraq, is a powerful expression of the anguish suffered by military personnel and civilians from both countries. Carol achieved the color palette by discharging canvas. She then scanned news articles and other imagery and enhanced them in Photoshop. Carol poses the questions, "Who are these people? Who have they left behind? What of the lives they will not have? This is to acknowledge them."

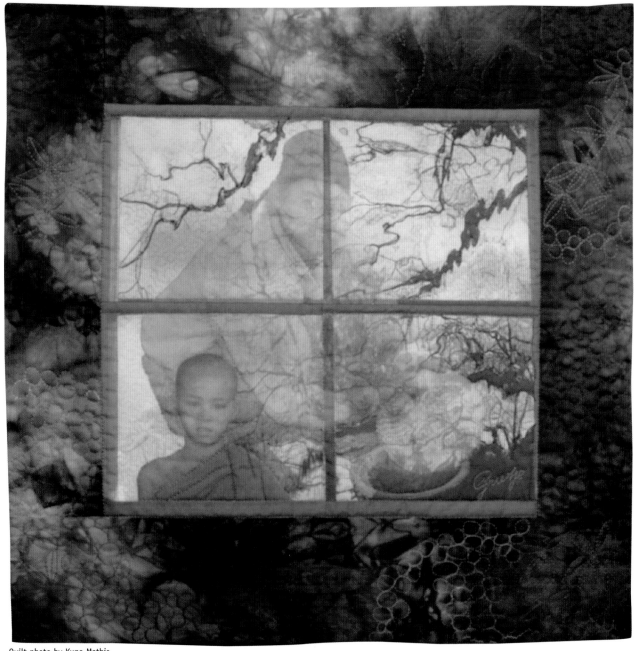

Quilt photo by Kuno Mathis

Burmese Days 2, Grietje van der Veen, Oberwil, Switzerland, 20˝ × 20˝

Grietje shot the photos in her quilt on a trip to "one of the most beautiful countries I have ever seen." A photograph of a boy monk and a girl washing dishes on the floor were scanned, then manipulated using Paint Shop Pro 9 and printed on cotton. Hand-dyed fabrics make up the borders.

Mount Koyasan: Ancestors, Arlé Sklar-Weinstein,
Hastings-on-Hudson, NY, 37¼˝ × 29½˝

Scans of slides, original artwork, and actual objects were
enlarged, tiled, and manipulated using Photoshop 7 and
CS2. Arlé heat transferred them onto fabric in mirror
image and combined them with sheer and solid fabrics
that were layered, quilted, embroidered, appliquéd, and
embellished with mixed media.

Oh! Oh! Busted!, Marjorie Post, Portland, OR, 18″ × 31″

Photos of the fields and farms in the Willamette Valley of Oregon were the source for this humorous wall-hanging. Marjorie first printed her images on paper, then cut and rearranged them to create her design. After printing the photos on white cotton, she sewed and quilted them onto batting and backing using a raw-edge technique with invisible thread. The freeform, unbound edges add to the casual reality of the design.

Rachet Wheel, Mary Tabar, San Diego, CA, 38″ × 29″

An old wheel leaning against a eucalyptus tree is the focal point in this quilt. Mary resized the photo in Photoshop, then printed it in 16 tiles (sections), using the *Poster* option on her printer. After sewing the sheets together, Mary cut the image every 5″ into diagonal strips, removed every other strip, then combined these with pieced strips that feature some of her hand-dyed fabrics.

Arroyo Seco Ride, Nicole Yardley, Longmont, CO, 34″ × 26″

Nicole's quilts are all about color in its many moods and expressions, a theme that is explored beautifully in this composition. She created the front part of the truck with fabrics, inks, and acrylic paints. The entire truck is machine trapuntoed. The fence, trees, tailgate, rack, side window, and rearview mirror were printed on cotton or silk enhanced with ink and acrylic paint. The trees/fence print was split in half, and a piece of white was added, then hand painted with sky and clouds.

No-One Knows, Laura Kemshall, Trysull Wolverhampton, United Kingdom, 63″ × 27″

One of a series of three quilts inspired by Laura's love of sketchbooks, this quilt features actual pages inserted in the seams of the main quilt. The images, edited with Paint Shop Pro, developed from the artist's studies of hedges and barbed wire fences. The fabrics were either hand dyed or hand painted, and surface decoration was done with discharge, drawing, and digital machine embroidery. Laura used heat-transfer paper for the digital images.

Ringo's Repose, Cyndy Lyle Rymer, Danville, CA, 35″ × 28″

A series of photos of Cyndy's cat finding a comfortable place to rest were enhanced and manipulated with filters in Photoshop Elements. And then sometimes serendipity steps in and lends a hand. In this case, when the fabric sheet started looking like it was going to jam in her 13″ × 19″ printer, Cyndy tugged it a bit to straighten it. The slight double image of the cat was the result. The smaller photos were printed on cotton and organza and layered in that order on the quilt top. Hand-dyed fabrics, including some geometric white tone-on-tone fabrics, were used for the borders, and the piece was hand and machine quilted.

Eddy, Laura Cater-Woods,
Billings, MT, 23″ × 17″

Frequent walks along the Yellowstone
River in her hometown of Billings,
Montana, provide Laura with a myriad
of images to explore in her artwork. She
manipulated the images using Photoshop
Elements, then printed them on pretreated silk. Free-motion embroidery,
quilting, and hand beading add to the
wonderful texture of this quilt.

Nothing Is Forever, Thom Atkins,
Santa Cruz, CA, 38″ × 59″

A photo of Angkor Thom taken by Lois Robin in
Cambodia was scanned, then manipulated in
Photoshop. Thom transposed parts of the image and
created part of the second head. Image Sharp printed
the 18″ × 25″ image on polyester velour. Thom cut up
the velour, hand-appliquéd it to a background, and
created a jungle around the heads with commercial
fabrics and re-colored silk leaves. He used permanent
markers and Prismacolor markers for additional color
and sewed glass beads on by hand.

Quilt photo by Holly Knott

Liberty One and Liberty Two 2, Holly Knott, Marcellus, NY, 24″ × 17″

Holly started with digital photographs that she took of the Liberty One and Liberty Two skyscrapers in Philadelphia. Because she photographed them looking up, the buildings appear wider at the bottom. This keystone effect emphasizes their incredible height. The artist continued that perspective by creating a quilt incorporating her photograph, which she sliced into three sections, with her hand-painted, hand-stamped fabrics. The fabrics look architectural themselves and extend the photograph into the quilt, blending reality into abstraction. She didn't want the photographs to look pasted on, but rather to be an extension of the fabric.

Ice Storm, Carol Soderlund, Geneva, NY, 36½″ × 36″

Carol used Photoshop CS to play with images taken during an ice storm. White cotton duck was pieced and patched, collaged with acrylic gel medium and paper prints, painted with acrylic paints and inks, layered with batting, and free-motion quilted. Carol compares the juxtaposition of seemingly soft snow with the icy coatings on tree branches to the soft canvas combined with crisp collaged paper in her quilt.

Asilomar Evenings, Sandra Hart, Los Gatos, CA, 24″ × 45″

Fourteen different photos taken on the grounds of the Asilomar Conference Center in Pacific Grove, California, were combined in Photoshop into two vertical collages joined with narrow sashing. The border is a digitally rendered progression of 1½″ squares of muted rainbow colors. These were printed on textured silk by Color Textiles, then quilted with a variety of decorative threads and couched fibers.

Imaginary Yellowstone,
Gudny Campbell, Monterey, CA,
$30\frac{1}{4}'' \times 37\frac{1}{4}''$

Gudny cropped, mirror imaged, and otherwise manipulated photos of Yellowstone in Photoshop Elements. Using Bubble Jet Set 2000, she prepared her own fabric and printed the photos on silk and cotton. These were then collaged to create an abstract version of the park. Fabric strips and yarns knitted together were photographed and also made part of the quilt, which was finally embellished with yarns and hand-painted silk ribbon.

Pawley's Island, Barbara Webster, Burnsville, NC, 52″ × 52″

Late afternoon proved to be a great time to take the photos of rippled sand that appear in the background and the medallions of this quilt. Barbara created the border from a photo of sea oats that grow on the dunes. She used CorelDRAW to design the quilt, which was machine pieced and hand appliquéd by Barbara and machine quilted by Rachel Reese. Photos were printed by Chris Moore with a Mimaki Dyejet printer using reactive dye.

Ash Splash, Charlotte Ziebarth, Boulder, CO, 56″ × 38″

Charlotte's work "blends fabrics and quilting with photography, digital design, and a love of nature." With white cotton fabric as the base, she paints, dyes, silk screens, and uses resists. She then interlayers these with inkjet-printed images. The photos are altered, then printed on an Epson 2200 extra-wide printer with pigment inks. Charlotte uses a collage style to create layered surfaces. Krylon acrylic ultraviolet filter is sprayed on the quilt at its completion as a final protective layer.

Translucent, Kerry McFall, Corvallis, OR, 32″ × 36″

With this quilt, Kerry makes a strong case for her belief that autumn in the Pacific Northwest is every bit as beautiful as the renowned East Coast colors of the season. This shot was taken outside Salem, Oregon, and enhanced in Photoshop. One border was created from an altered image of a Broken Dishes quilt Kerry had made. The images were printed by Thom Bach on a large-format printer. Kerry added tulle to the leaves in several places to make it look like they overlap the border. A glaze of acrylic paint thinned with fabric medium was applied over the background.

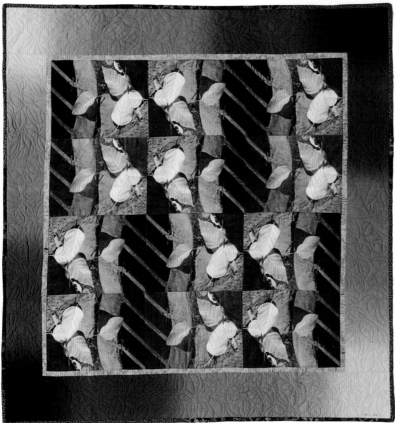

Yellow Leaves on Grate, Marina Salume, Half Moon Bay, CA, 37½″ × 38″

Marina printed several copies of the same image on pretreated cotton sheeting. Flipping and rearranging the images helped create secondary images. Commercial or hand-dyed fabrics were used for the borders, and quilting was done with invisible thread.

Quilt photo by Barbara Barrick McKie

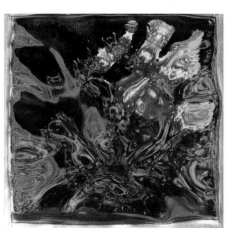

Dahlia Reflections #2, Barbara Barrick McKie, Lyme, CT, 42½″ × 42½″

Barbara's garden is full of one of her favorite flowers— beautifully huge (larger than 10″ blooms) dahlias. One image of dahlias was combined and manipulated in Photoshop CS with a reflection of the flowers in a glass brick. Barbara then printed them on an Epson 4000 printer with SubliJet IQ disperse dye inks onto Accuplot paper. She then used a heat press to transfer it to white polyester crepe fabric. Check out her technique on *Simply Quilts*, episode 1134.

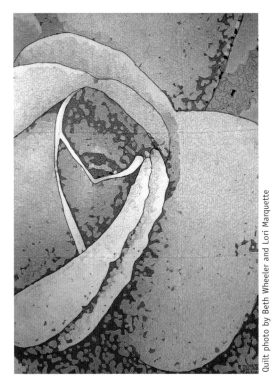

Quilt photo by Beth Wheeler and Lori Marquette

Lost in Silk, Beth Wheeler and Lori Marquette, Fort Wayne, IN, 22¹⁄₂″ × 31″

Anemones, Daphne Greig, North Saanich, British Columbia, Canada, 16¹⁄₄″ × 18″

The Japanese anemones pictured in this quilt grow just outside Daphne's studio and keep her company while she quilts. Using Photoshop Elements, Daphne adjusted the color of one close-up of the center and maintained the original color of another full flower image. Hand-dyed, hand-painted, and commercial fabrics sewn in string fashion surround the printed images.

Quilt photo by Beth Wheeler and Lori Marquette

Iris Fantasy, Beth Wheeler and Lori Marquette, Fort Wayne, IN, 23¹⁄₂″ × 28³⁄₄″

After many years in the quilting, crafting, and publishing industries, Beth and Lori joined forces to form Two Sipsters Studio, creating works of art by altering photos with photo-editing software such as Photoshop. The images are printed on fabric with an inkjet printer and pigment inks, and are then free-motion quilted to add dimension, texture, and definition.

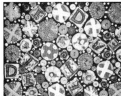

Cup Mandala, Therese May, San Jose, CA, 65˝ × 75˝

An original pen-and-ink drawing, coupled with a desire to see how many of Therese's own fabric designs could be used in a quilt, were the starting point for this amazing quilt. The Pixeladies—Deb Cashatt and Kris Sazaki (see page 91)—enlarged and printed the original drawing on cotton. They also printed the 8˝ × 10˝ border panels. The borders started as fabric embellished with polymer clay, buttons, acrylic paint, and fabric paint. The original quilting design was programmed into and then quilted with a longarm by Carlos Ramirez of Ohana Quilt Company.

To See a World in a Grain of Sand, Rosalind Aylmer, West Vancouver, British Columbia, Canada, 31″ × 57″

Rosalind incorporated devoré patterning (similar to velvet burnout) through screen printing, in addition to screen printing with dyes, pigments, and puff medium; hand dyeing; and digital printing. Images and text were hand drawn or based on copyright-free images, then manipulated using Adobe's Photo Deluxe Home Edition, and finally transferred to process screens. The footprint photo was printed on silk prepared with Bubble Jet Set 2000.

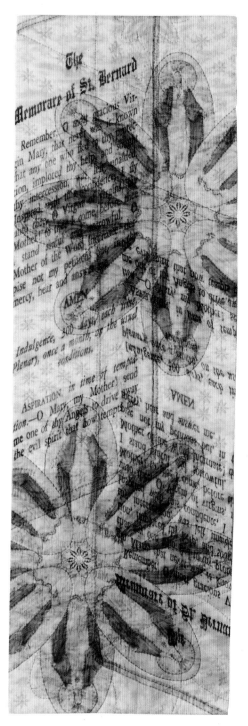

Mary Daisy, Janine LeBlanc, Raleigh, NC, 16″ × 49″

A digital scan of a childhood image was manipulated in Photoshop CS2, then sent to TC2 in Cary, North Carolina, to be printed on a Stork wide-format printer. Janine is a fan of layers—"both real and computerized"—in which images are stacked like layers on a cake and, as a result, "interact with each other and create new meaning."

Sorensen's Scarf, Pixeladies, Cameron Park, CA, 16″ × 81″

Deb Cashatt and Kris Sazaki, or the Pixeladies, spent a glorious fall day at Sorensen's Resort near Lake Tahoe, California, with friends whose average age was 78. The photos, along with a map of the area, were collaged in Photoshop CS and printed on silk habotai using Jacquard silk dyes. The fabric was steamed to set the dyes.

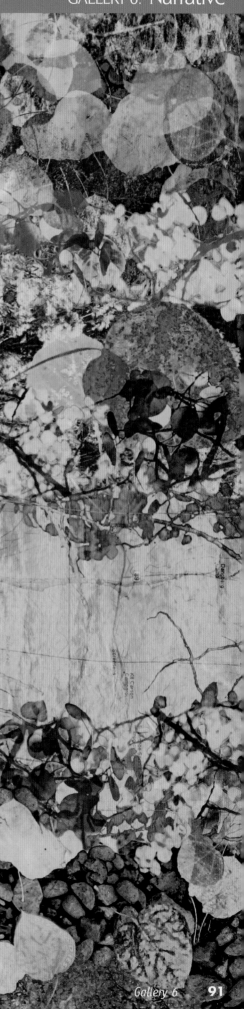

Appendix

Additional Photoshop Elements tools

- **Eyedropper tool** Use this to sample and copy colors. Helpful when you are painting with the *Paint Bucket* tool (see page 38).

- **Lasso tool** This tool allows you to draw around items within your image and then either cut out the selected area completely or copy and paste/move the selected area to a new file or a new spot in the existing image. Try the *Magnetic Lasso tool* first. (There is actually a magnet in the icon, so it's easy to figure out which one to use.) The *Magnetic Lasso* grabs the edges of whatever it is you are trying to select. Just click and drag around the image, clicking every so often to set anchor points. When you reach the point where you started and click, the image will be lassoed. At this point, you can delete your selection or move it to a new file or within the existing image file.

Tip

Use the Backspace key on your keyboard to go backward to the previous anchor when using the *Magnetic Lasso tool.*

- **Magic Wand tool** Use this tool to select parts of an image based on color. Read about it in the Photoshop Elements *Help* file.

Need More Information?

When you need more information about a tool, type the name of it into the box in the upper-right corner of the screen next to the question mark. A new screen will appear that explains how to use the tool.

- **Type tool** Add text with this tool, then play with the text to your heart's content. Use the options in the menu bar to select font, size, and style. Use the *Move tool* to place it where you want it. Experiment with *Layer>Type>Warp Text* for ways to bend and shape text to fit the content.

Warped text is fun to apply.

- **Cookie Cutter tool** You can get really cute with this cropping tool. Select *Shape* and *Shape Options* from the menu bar and crop away.

Tip

When selecting the cookie cutter shape, the solid shapes will crop the shape shown. The open shapes will crop an outline of that shape.

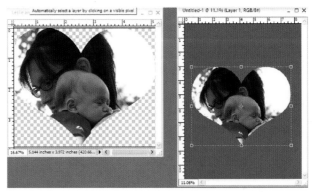

Use a solid cookie cutter, open a new blank file, use the *Paint Bucket tool* to color in the background, then move the image onto its new background.

- **Straighten tool** Use this to straighten crooked images.

- **Red Eye tool** Gets the red out of eyes in photos taken with a flash.

- **Healing Brush tool** A bit tricky to use successfully, but it does get rid of unwanted spots and blemishes.

- **Clone Stamp tool** Use this tool to get rid of "undesirables" in your image (see page 50).

Original photo

The extra swimmer is gone, courtesy of the *Clone Stamp tool*.

- **Eraser tool** This tool does just what is says—it erases. When you are using *Layers* (see page 18), this tool removes the top layer to reveal what lies in the layers beneath.

- **Paint Bucket tool** Pouring color into or on an image is encouraged with this sometimes surprising—meaning a bit more difficult to control—tool. Choose a color, then click on the image. This works well if you want a colored background in a new file. You may need to repeat the action several times if the image is "fussy," such as when you want to change the color of foliage.

- **Gradient tool** A cousin of the *Paint Bucket tool,* this cool tool offers a selection of graduated background colors in a variety of effects.

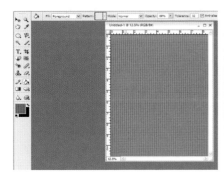

Create a colored background with the *Paint Bucket tool.*

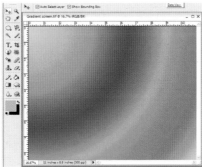

Printed on fabric, this could almost be tie-dyed, thanks to the *Gradient tool.*

- **Shape tools** Draw a variety of shapes or choose from the many stock shapes available from the drop-down menu.

Add shapes around parts of your image.

- **Blur, Sharpen, and Smudge tools** They all do what they say, working to change parts of your image.

- **Sponge, Dodge, and Burn tools** These are hand-me-down tools from photographers who used to spend hours in their darkrooms trying to fix their print-from-film photos. Think of using the *Sponge tool* when you want to make a small part of your image more or less colorful.

Resources

All-in-Ones/Printers

Check your local office-supply or discount-warehouse store or look online at

Canon Company
www.canon.com

Epson Company
www.epson.com

Hewlett-Packard Company
www.hp.com

Pretreated Fabric Sheets

ColorPlus Inkjet Fabrics by Color Textiles
Many different fabrics, including poplin, broadcloth, denim, and silks in sheets and rolls
www.colortextiles.com

EQ Printables by Electric Quilt
Cotton sheets up to 13″ × 19″
www.electricquilt.com

Inkjet Printable Fabric by The Vintage Workshop
Fabric sheets and images and projects on CD
www.thevintageworkshop.com

Inkjet Printing Sheets by Jacquard
Cotton, silk, and ExtravOrganza sheets
www.jacquardproducts.com

Natural Miracle Fabric Sheets by C. Jenkins Necktie & Chemical Co.
Fabric in sheets and by the yard
www.cjenkinscompany.com

Printed Treasures by Milliken
Cotton sheets in sew-in, iron-in, and peel-and-stick
www.printedtreasures.com

Collage Sheets and Ephemera

Art Chix Studio
www.artchixstudio.com

B-muse Products
www.b-muse.com

Picturetrail
www.picturetrail.com/lostartcreations

Stampington & Company
www.stampington.com

Tallulahs
www.tallulahs.com

Vintage Image Madness
www.vintageimagemadness.com

Software

Adobe Photoshop Elements
www.adobe.com

Corel Paint Shop Pro Photo XI, Painter Essentials 3
www.corel.com

Kaleidoscope Kreator
www.kaleidoscopecollections.com

PhotoMontage, Panorama Maker, Collage Creator
www.arcsoft.com

Print Shop
www.broderbund.com

Photo Storage and Sharing Sites

www.pictures.aol.com
www.pixagogo.com
www.smugmug.com

Fabric Printing

Daydreams Art Fabric
Rebecca Martinez/John Potter
PO Box 1358
Colfax, CA 95713
www.colfaxcloth.com
530-346-7160

Inkdrop Printing
A Division of [TC]²
211 Gregson Drive
Cary, NC 27511
www.inkdropprinting.com

Silicon Gallery Fine Arts Print Ltd.
139 N. 3rd Street
Philadelphia, PA 19106
215-238-6062
www.fineartprint.com

Pixeladies
4061 Flying C Road
Cameron Park, CA 95682
916-320-8774
www.pixeladies.com
info@pixeladies.com

Starforest Quilts
www.starforestquilts.com
barbara@starforestquilts.com

Patterns

Make It Easy Sewing & Crafts
Royal Gems by Toby Lischko (page 64) is available from www.quiltwoman.com

Books

Altered Photo Artistry, Beth Wheeler with Lori Marquette, C&T Publishing, Lafayette, CA, 2007

Beautifully Embellished Landscapes, Joyce Becker, C&T Publishing, Lafayette, CA, 2006

Luscious Landscapes, Joyce Becker, C&T Publishing, Lafayette, CA, 2003

More Photo Fun, The Hewlett-Packard Company with Cyndy Lyle Rymer and Lynn Koolish, C&T Publishing, Lafayette, CA, 2005

Photo Fun, The Hewlett-Packard Company, edited by Cyndy Lyle Rymer, C&T Publishing, Lafayette, CA, 2004

Quilted Memories, Lesley Riley, Sterling Publishing, New York, 2005

Magazines

Adobe Photoshop Elements Techniques
www.photoshopelementsuser.com

Creative TECHniques
www.creativetechniquesmag.com

Quilting Arts and *Cloth Paper Scissors*
www.quiltingarts.com

Somerset Memories (formerly Legacy)
www.stampington.com

About the Authors

An amateur photographer before she was a quilter, Cyndy Lyle Rymer now spends as much time getting lost in Photoshop Elements as she does quilting. Cyndy was an editor at C&T Publishing, but jumped the fence to write a novel (in progress) and work at a local quilt store. She loves teaching all the magical things that can be done with an inkjet printer, with or without a computer.

Lynn Koolish is an eclectic quilter, teacher, and author. She works in a variety of styles and loves experimenting with new ideas, materials, and techniques. She works full-time editing quilting books and teaches a variety of surface design and quilting classes. Her quilts have appeared in books, magazines, and local and national quilt shows.

Also by Cyndy Lyle Rymer

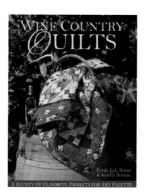

Also by Lynn Koolish

More books on Inkjet printing on fabric

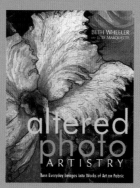

The Hewlett-Packard Company, edited by Cyndy Lyle Rymer

The Hewlett-Packard Company with Cyndy Lyle Rymer and Lynn Koolish

Beth Wheeler with Lori Marquette

Index